The Co
By Bru

Copyright © 07/12/2010

Preface

What do you believe about Christianity? What about the Bible? Do you believe its God's Word or a work of man? Everyone needs to examine his or herself on these questions – especially if they claim to be a Christian, because no one should claim any specific belief without something to base it on.

If you're unsure of your position on these questions I hope that this book will help you resolve that issue. Let me begin with scripture, which without it a Christian really has no basis of belief, and no hope of knowing Jesus Christ on an intimate level.

The Holy Bible is the greatest book ever written, or should I say collection of books, and it's very unfortunate that there are so many people who do not realize this. It's not great because of the clever penmanship of man, but because of the supernatural inspiration of our creator. God saw to it that we would have this special revelation in order for us to know him on a more intimate basis.

Great literature is hailed by scholars and commoners alike all over the world, yet critics come out of the woodwork in many forms when the mere title of this great book is mentioned. Why do you think this is so? There is one name that sums up the answer to this question... SATAN. The great deceiver, commonly known as "Satan" or "the devil" is *against* everything God is *for*, and he is always looking for ways to denounce God's word and paint an erroneous caricature of Jesus Christ. He hates God and knows that he, along with humanity will be judged according to God's word and therefore wants to take as many down with him as he can. There are many people willing to help him with this task by openly and publicly displaying their dissent – usually by taking things out of context in order to convince others that the Bible is fallible and full of contradictions. He is always whispering in the ears of those who will listen, and believe me there is no shortage of willing listeners. We are all at risk of falling for his lies, temptations, and misdirection, because we are human, however, for those of us who have been saved by God's grace, we can put on the "whole armor of God" as described in Ephesians chapter 6:10-20. One of those pieces of armor is the Sword of the Spirit - which is the Word of God - which is the Holy Bible.

As 2 Timothy 3:16-17 states, "All scripture is given by inspiration of God, and is profitable for doctrine, for reproof, for correction, for instruction in righteousness: That the man of God may be perfect, thoroughly furnished unto all good works". This is a wonderful verse of scripture stating that whatever our spiritual need is, the Word of God is adequate to supply that need. This is not to say that every question man can come up with will be addressed, because the Bible isn't a scientific, historic, or mathematic text book, even though it's accuracy in these fields is verified when real science, history, and logic are applied. God's concern is for our spiritual health, and even though many life questions can be answered by God's word, his main focus has always been to reconcile a lost and dying world unto himself. Because of this, anyone studying God's word will notice a common theme throughout scripture, and that is history of creation and culture, history of our fall from grace, and God's plan of salvation – everything centering on Jesus Christ.

Some question the relevance of the Bible in the present times, calling it archaic, but what many fail to realize is that the Bible is *alive,* and has been shown over and over again to be extremely relevant. Of course this is not to say that the Bible lives and breathes in the physical sense…that would be absurd, but because scripture is God breathed, its relevance is supernatural. Anyone willing to engulf themselves in God's word will find that it is timeless and extremely applicable to the present world, as well as, past and future.

As Hebrews 4:12 states "For the word of God is quick, and powerful, and sharper than any two edged sword, piercing even to the dividing asunder of soul and spirit, and of the joints and marrow, and is a discerner of the thoughts and intents of the heart." This is saying that God's word is far from archaic and so powerful that it can reach into the depths of a person's mind. It's able to slice away any faux persona and expose his or her very thoughts and intents. The "thoughts of the heart" is referring to your core being, or how you really feel no matter what you may project to others. I know some will read this and find themselves automatically rejecting the authority and accuracy of scripture because of presuppositions they may or may not have made explicit to themselves, but I challenge them first to be honest with themselves and read this with unbiased intent, and second, truly allow the words of the Bible to be savored by their mind. I feel that they will be surprised just how alive the Word is, and how it will relate to their very existence.

The Bible tells us about God's character and what he deems important. It lets us know why things are the way they are, and in essence gives us the perfect standard to live by. Some refuse the Bible because it is full of *rules* and *boundaries*, which impose on their lifestyle, but rules and boundaries are there to protect us just like traffic laws are there to protect drivers and their passengers. The rules and boundaries in God's word are there to protect us from the consequences of sin. We have to trust God, because he knows what is best for us in the long run. Seek God while he may be found, because a day is coming when the last soul will be saved, and time shall be no more.

I, like everyone else, have made many mistakes in my life, but I have also learned many lessons as a result of those mistakes. There is one mistake in particular that I wish I had learned from sooner than I did, and the mistake I speak of is not pursuing a relationship with God and seeking his wisdom much earlier in life. I allowed disappointments while witnessing to my friends as a child to crush my desire to continue witnessing. I started drifting away from God for what now seems like an eternity, and I was introduced to my own selfish nature. If I had used this disappointment to *fuel* my desire instead, who knows where I'd be now. The good thing is that, as long as you're alive, it's not too late to start anew.

The task of being a pastor, teacher, evangelist, or missionary is not the purpose of every Christian, some are called to these duty's, and others are called to different things, but spreading the gospel of Jesus Christ is something every born again believer should do, and if a person is truly saved they will have a desire in their heart to share Jesus with everyone they meet, because we are to love one another, and loving someone means that you do whatever it takes to care for their well-being.

I know this may sound a little strange, but this story started as a result of depression. I have had bouts of depression for a while and, like many others, had no idea of the cause. In talking with others about this, it was suggested to me many times to go to a doctor and ask for anti-depressants. While there are many out there who have genuine medical conditions that require this type of action, I couldn't help feeling that I was not one of those people, and treating the symptom instead of the problem wasn't going to fix anything. The problem was that I had turned away from God, and lost the joy of my salvation. It took longer than it should have to sink in, but I finally realized that I hadn't gone to the only one who could fix my problem. I had relied totally on myself, and had been living selfishly as well, but God was waiting patiently for me to come back and ask him for help. There are people out there who look at Christians, and God alike, to be force-full and overbearing, which I hate to say but *some Christians are*, however, God does not force himself on us. He patiently waits for us to get the picture, and come to him. He uses all kinds of situations to get our attention, and sometimes these situations are very uncomfortable, and maybe even painful, but he does this because he *loves* us and wants the best for all human kind. Parents who love their children discipline their children, and guide them, not because they want to hurt them or keep them from experiencing a full life, but just the opposite. The same can be said about our Lord, who is the ultimate father, and very qualified I might add since he designed the family institution. When I finally got out of the way of myself, and asked God what he wanted for my life instead of carving my own path, it was as if someone turned on the light switch that had been eluding me for so long, and I knew that it was time to start developing a real relationship with God – one that would put him first in my life, and ultimately give me peace, and purpose in my life.

The story that is contained on the following pages came from this journey to know my savior and is based on reality. The character names are fictitious, as well as, the locations and order of events, but the questions, answers, and scripture references are very real. I have answered all questions using scripture found in the King James Version of the Bible, along with information from Christian and non-Christian books and articles, and I hope anyone who reads this will look up these scriptures in their own bibles, and do some research themselves, not just take my word for it.

My desire when this work is complete is to have learned more about God's character myself, and hopefully help someone else answer some questions in the process. If only one person is brought into a relationship with Jesus Christ, then this has been worth every minute.

Chapter 1
Car trouble

    The quaint city of Blue Ridge is comfortably nestled between the beautiful mountains of north Georgia. It's been a privilege to call this home for nearly 50 years now, and its beauty never ceases to amaze me. I moved here from Florida when I was 20 years old, and believe me I don't miss the heat and energy draining humidity one bit.

    My name is Jack Miller, but most folks around here just call me grandpa; I guess that could have something to do with all this grey hair I've accumulated over the years.

    I worked as a train engineer for various railroads until I retired four years ago, and I guess that's what drew me to this place; the Blue Ridge Scenic Railway is located right in the middle of town if I ever get the sudden urge for a ride.

    I always loved passing through these small towns late at night – seeing how peaceful everything looked as the homes and businesses slept, however, during the day it's a different story. When everything wakes up, the streets fill with cars loaded with people rushing to get to work, and other various destinations, then as the day progresses, the sidewalks follow suit.

    You've probably heard the saying, "everybody knows everybody when you live in a small town" and that is so true. Once you've been here a few years, everyone knows all about you. Some may not like that, but I find a certain comfort in it, and so did Shirley. The Lord took her home almost nine years ago, and she adored this town right till the end, even though the cancer made her final days and nights much more painful than she would have liked. Shirley and I bought this little house on Main Street back in the fall of 1960 when we moved here. We liked it because of its prime location near the center of town, and we could sit on the front porch for hours reading, and people watching. I miss her tremendously, but I know that one day when my turn comes, we will spend eternity together with Jesus, and there will be no more pain, cancer, or any of the many ailments suffered by people here on earth. We'll both have new bodies and a new home, as the old hymn goes.

There are a lot of people that don't have the same *peace* and *security* that Shirley and I shared. God has manifested himself to everyone, but we have the ability to suppress that knowledge and go our own way, which really is a miserable existence when you get down to it. It's possible to go through life pretending that there is nothing to worry about, and death is the end, but somewhere buried deep within is the knowledge that this philosophy is wrong. Sure they say nice things at the funerals like, "He or she is in a better place" or, "We'll see them again some day" or even, "He or she was a good person and now they're at peace" but the truth is, unless they've been born again, they really don't know, because they haven't lived by Gods word and accepted Jesus Christ as their Savior....instead, they have lived for themselves and are hoping for the best. Romans 5:1 states, "Therefore being justified by faith, we have peace with God through our Lord Jesus Christ." And Isaiah 48:22 says, "There is no peace, saith the Lord, unto the wicked." So I'm very glad Shirley and I are in the "justified" category.

Since her death, and my retirement, I have carried on the daily traditions we shared when I wasn't out riding the rails. I get up in the morning – prepare a pot of coffee and a small breakfast, usually consisting of some oatmeal, or cereal, or maybe a bagel with cream cheese, then make my way out to the front porch to read the paper, and watch the town come alive. The fact that this story took place in September made things even better, because there was a hint of fall in the air, and it reminded me of the day we moved into this house.

The week I speak of happened to be a lot busier than normal, because there were fall festivals going on all around, and people had come from all over to check out the festivities, and enjoy the mountain scenery. I thought I would check things out for myself, and say hello to some of the town folk....and the visitors of course, but it was Wednesday and I definitely wanted to get back home in time to get ready for church. Shirley and I always loved Wednesday night Bible study. It gave us another excuse to engulf ourselves in Gods word with our brethren, as if we needed an excuse.

When we moved here we searched for a long time to find the right church. It had to be a church that focused on true Biblical teaching and preaching, and not on membership, or "tickling the ears" of the congregation in order to try and make everyone happy. There are many churches today that have taken God out, and filled the void with everything you can imagine – basically stating that man can do it better. To me they seem a lot like pep rallies instead of church services. The funny thing is they still can't move people like the Holy Spirit can when God is at the center of a church, no matter how hard they try – and they never will!

Sorry about that, I got a little side tracked there; now where was I? Oh yes, the search for a church. After lots of visiting we came across a little church that was truly God sent. It is located in-between Blairsville and Blue Ridge – off the beaten path – and only a short drive from home.

I don't want you to think there are no good churches here in town, because there are, but we knew we were home when we walked through the doors the first time; from the singing to the preaching, and the fellowship of its members, God was definitely there, and so were we every time the doors opened.

The ride to church is a little lonelier now without Shirley with me, but when I get there I'm truly with my family. That church has always made members and visitors alike feel comfortable and at home, which is how God wants his family to be toward one another. Fellowship is a major component when it comes to growing, and maturing in Christ, so we must love and respect one another, and be of one spirit. As Paul said in Philippians 1:27, "Only let your conversation be as it becometh the gospel of Christ: that whether I come and see you, or else be absent, I may hear of your affairs, that ye stand fast in one spirit, with one mind striving together for the faith of the gospel;" If a church is not of one accord, division and trouble are inevitable.

I was looking forward to that night's service, but it was still early so I decided since there was time to spare, I would check out the festival, and as I was getting ready to head into town, something caught my attention as I walked past the living room window. There were two people standing in my driveway, and I couldn't help but notice they were fanning smoke away from their faces. Fire was the first thing that came to mind, so I rushed into the kitchen - grabbed the fire extinguisher – and headed out the front door. Thankfully I didn't see any flames, but there was quite a bit of smoke coming from underneath this beautifully restored, silver late 1970's model Jeep Renegade. I could appreciate the work that had gone into this beautiful vehicle, since I had been a jeep enthusiast myself a few years back. The young man looked like he was in his early twenties, as well as the young woman with him. They both had dark brown hair and were dressed casually in shorts, t-shirts, and flip-flops so I assumed they were probably here for the festival.

"Looks like you kids are having a little trouble." I said as I walked down the driveway toward them.

"I believe your right." The young man said, as he continued to fan the smoke. "I think something is wrong with the transmission; it started making a loud whining noise just before the smoke began billowing out, which prompted my decision to pull off the road."

"Well, after this smoke clears, we'll have a look and see what the problem is." I said as I reached out to shake his hand. "My name is Jack Miller - I live here."

"Nice to meet you Mr. Miller - I'm Tim Conley and this is my wife Carmen." He said as he gestured toward the young lady.

"I'm sorry we're blocking your driveway, but it's a pleasure to meet you." Carmen said with a smile.

"Oh that's quite alright; no one ever plans for these things to happen, and besides, I'm not going anywhere until later this evening." I said reassuringly. "It looks like the smoke is letting up some. Do you mind if I have a look?" I asked.

"Be my guest." Tim answered, "I never have been very mechanically inclined."

"That's an understatement." Carmen added with a laugh.

"He didn't ask for your opinion." Tim said, as he playfully put his hand over Carmen's mouth.

I got down on my knees and looked under the jeep, knowing that it probably wasn't going to be good news, and there it was; a crack in the transmission housing was allowing fluid to leak out onto the exhaust pipe.

"I'm afraid this is going to take more expertise than we have." I said as I painfully got back to my feet...old age does that to you.

"What did you see?" Tim asked.

I explained the crack and suggested he call a tow truck.

"I'll call roadside assistance." Carmen said, as she reached into her purse for her cell phone.

She flipped open the phone, and I could see the distress on her face as she pushed buttons, which apparently weren't yielding the results she had anticipated.

"I can't believe this." She said with obvious aggravation, "The battery is completely dead; it won't even light up."

"Why don't you kids come up to the house and you can use my phone." I offered.

"I hate to impose on you any more than we already have," Carmen said. "But we sure would appreciate it."

"Oh don't you worry about it one bit, your not imposing on me at all." I said smiling at the two of them. "We all need help every now and then, and who knows, one day I could break down in front of your house, and you can help me."

We walked up the short driveway and I opened the front door – motioning them to go on in.

"The phone is over by the sofa, so make yourself comfortable, and call whoever you need to." I said, pointing at the end table next to the sofa.

"Thank you Mr. Miller." She said, as she sat down next to the phone.

"No need to call me mister, I'm still young at heart; just call me Jack."

"Ok Jack, thank you very much for being so kind." She said, smiling in the midst of aggravation.

"While she's calling for help, can I get you kid's something to drink?" I asked. "I have water, sweet tea, lemonade, and a few sodas."

"Sweet tea would be great." Tim replied. "We both love sweet tea."

"You two must be from the south." I stated inquisitively, as I walked toward the kitchen. "Loving sweet tea just happens to be a prerequisite to live here."

"We live just outside Atlanta in the town of Mableton." Tim replied, nodding in agreement with my observation while following me into the kitchen.

After placing the fire extinguisher back in its rightful place, I took three glasses from the cupboard, filled them with ice, and placed them on the counter.

"The tow truck is on the way." Carmen said, coming into the kitchen behind us. "They should be here in just a few minutes; apparently there is a jeep dealership just outside of town."

"Oh yes." I said as I filled the glasses. "They're just three or four miles up the four-lane so it shouldn't take them long. Until then we can sit on the front porch and enjoy our drinks."

"Thank you so much Jack; I guess we picked the right house to break down in front of." Tim said, as he handed Carmen a glass, and picked up one for hisself.

We walked out on the porch and the two of them sat down in the swing while I took a seat in my favorite rocker.

"So what brings you kid's to Blue Ridge? Are you here for the festival?" I asked.

"Actually we didn't know anything about the festival." Carmen replied. "We rented a cabin in Gatlinburg, Tennessee for a week, but check in is not till Friday afternoon, so we decided to leave early and spend tonight somewhere around here, and tomorrow night in Cherokee, North Carolina or something."

"That was the plan anyway." Tim interjected. "I guess things might be a little different now."

"Plans do have a tendency to change without warning sometimes, but as long as you keep a positive attitude, you can still have a good time." I said smiling. "That's a lesson I wish I'd learned when I was a kid, because it sure would have saved me a lot of heartache."

"You seem like a very positive person." Carmen said.

"Well I have a lot to be positive about, and besides, we only hurt ourselves when we look at life in a negative way."

"This is very true." Tim stated.

We chatted back and forth for a while until our attention was suddenly drawn to the street as we heard the sound of a large truck approaching.

"Well it looks like your ride is here." I said. "If you're finished with your drinks, just put them on the rail and I'll take care of them while you attend to the business at hand."

"Thanks again for your hospitality, Jack. I hope we get a chance to return the favor some day." Carmen said as she and Tim extended their hands for a fair well shake.

I shook their hands and said, "Just help someone else in need sometime, and consider the favor returned."

"You got it." She said as they walked away.

I took the glasses and went back inside to the kitchen so I could wash them, and I thought to myself how nice the two of them seemed, and it reminded me of how I felt about Shirley when we were that age. That night I would say a special prayer for them, and ask God to help them be as happy as we were.

I didn't know at that time that my experience with Tim and Carmen was just beginning, but I'm sure you've heard the saying, "The Lord works in mysterious ways." And he certainly does; Apparently there was more that needed to be said to the Conley's, and it's funny how the Lord will make sure everyone is in the right place at the right time, so his will is done. As Christians we need to be aware of this so when an opportunity arises to glorify God by leading someone to Christ, we need to step up to that duty.

I was just placing the glasses back into the cupboard, when I heard someone knocking at the front door, so I headed back that way, and through the window I could see Carmen standing there.

"Well hello again." I said as I opened the door. "Is everything ok?"

"I'm so sorry to bother you again," She said. "But it seems we have a little problem; the driver says he only has room for one person to ride with him, because of some damage to his seat, so can I use your phone again to call a taxi or something?"

I could see that she sincerely felt like she was imposing on me, judging by the look on her face, so I couldn't resist a little joke to break the tension.

"I'm sorry, but no you can't." I said as I watched her face change to this confused....I'm not sure what to say expression, and after a short pause I said, "But I'll be glad to give you a ride over there instead."

Her face then relaxed and a smile slowly began to appear as she realized I was just kidding with her. She gave a little laugh and said, "You really had me going there; I didn't know what to say to that."

"I'm sorry." I apologized. "I couldn't help myself, so the least I can do is give you kids a ride."

"We would really appreciate it, and we'll pay for your gas."

"Oh no, that's not necessary." I said. "It'll be my privilege to take you, and it's not that far. Let me get my keys and I'll meet you at my car."

"Thank you so much." She said as she walked off the porch toward Tim.

After grabbing my keys, and locking up the house, I walked out to the carport where they were both waiting on me, and I noticed the roll-back had their jeep loaded, and was starting to pull out of the driveway.

"Ya'll hop in, the doors are unlocked." I said, as I opened the driver side door, and got in myself.

I started the engine, and put the car in gear, as Tim began apologizing once again for being an inconvenience, but I held up my hand in a gesture to stop, and said, "Please, no more apologizing; you kids are not bothering me at all, and I don't have anywhere else I'm supposed to be right now."

We followed the tow truck to the nearby dealership, and I got out accompanying them to the service department waiting room.

"You don't have to stay here with us." Carmen said.

"You've done enough already, and we don't want to take any more of your time. If they can't get it fixed today, we'll get a hotel and rental car or something."

"No problem." I said, "I'll just hang out until you get some arrangements made, then I'll feel better about leaving."

"Ok." Carmen said, "But if you need to leave at any time, please do so alright."

"Deal." I said.

I walked on over to the seating area, and picked up the latest home improvement magazine while I waited for them to get their situation worked out. It was only about an hour until closing time, so I knew the jeep wouldn't get fixed that day, and they realized this too, because Carmen was at the counter with a phone book, calling out phone numbers of hotels, and rental car companies for Tim to call.

About ten minutes till six one of the service technicians came in and asked them to accompany him back to the shop; I assumed he was explaining to them the work that would have to be done, in order to get them going again.

A few minutes later Tim and Carmen reappeared, both with concerned looks on their faces.

"I take it the news wasn't good." I said.

Tim looked at me, shaking his head and said, "They say it's probably going to be two days before they can get another transmission, because no one around here has one for this early of a model."

"Well maybe they'll get it in time for you to make your check in time on Friday." I said, trying to show them a little optimism.

"That's the least of our problems." Carmen said, "We have called every hotel and Rental-Car Company within twenty miles, and there is nothing available, because of the festivals going on all around. Do you have any suggestions?" She asked.

"I sure do." I said, noticing how a little more cheerful expression appeared on their faces. "Why don't you kids stay with me; I have an extra room, and I would love to have the company....best of all it won't cost you a thing."

"We can't ask you to do that." Carmen stated.

"You're not asking, I'm offering; there's a difference, and besides, my feelings will be hurt if you don't accept." I replied.

"How can we say no to that?" Tim said with a smile.

"I guess you're right; I just don't want to be any trouble." Carmen said.

"It's no trouble at all, and besides, the Lord teaches us to be good Samaritans, and Jesus said one of the two greatest commandments was Thou shalt love thy neighbor as thyself."

"You've definitely been a good Samaritan." Tim stated, as he started back towards the shop again. "I'm just going to grab a few things from my jeep and I'll meet you guys at your car."

"Make sure you get my black bag!" Carmen exclaimed, "Without my makeup I'll be hideous tomorrow morning."

After retrieving a few things from his jeep, we left the dealership, and headed out. As we pulled into my driveway, a few minutes later, I realized it was six thirty, and it was time to get ready for church services, which start at seven thirty, so I helped them get settled into their room, and as I was walking back towards my room I turned and said,

"If you kids want to accompany me to church this evening, you are more than welcome; I would love to have you, and so would everyone else."

"Thanks for the offer, but I think we're going to walk into town and check out the festival since we're here for a while." Carmen answered.

"That sounds like fun." I said, "I think you've earned a little play time after all you've been through today."

After changing clothes I walked into the living room, where they were both sitting, and they immediately stood up which made me think, maybe they had changed their minds about going with me.

"Did you change your mind?" I asked.

"No, we just decided to leave whenever you did, because we didn't want to stay here without you." Carmen replied.

"Oh, don't worry about that." I said, "You kids just make yourselves at home, and leave whenever you're ready. There's food in the fridge, or several good restaurants downtown, so try to enjoy yourselves."

They followed me out anyway, so I locked the front door and placed my key under the welcome mat. "I should be home around nine or so, but if you get home before me, the key is right here."

"Thank you again for your kindness Jack." Carmen said smiling, "And I guess we'll see you around nine."

As I pulled out of the driveway, I saw them in my rearview mirror, walking towards town hand in hand, and I couldn't help but feel that the Lord had brought these two into my life for some reason, but at that point I just didn't know what that reason was. Everything happens for a purpose, even if we never understand what that purpose is, but just knowing that God is in control is so comforting for a Christian. We know that all things will work out according to his will.

We had a great Bible study that night, and the witness of the Holy Spirit was there in a mighty way. Our pastor preached about the end of time, and although there are people in the world that don't think it's appropriate to talk about this, because it scares them, we love to talk about it, because for Christians it means the beginning of an eternity with our Lord and Savior, and that's something to be happy about. I look forward to the day when I can see the one who gave his life as payment for my sins, so that I could have eternal life with him.

There is no need for a Christian to worry about these things once you put this short life in prospective with eternity. For those who are scared of the end, maybe they don't understand this, or maybe they've never been saved. Whatever the reason, it's extremely important to examine ourselves and make sure that we are ready for that day. Philippians 4:7 states, "And the peace of God, which passeth all understanding, shall keep your hearts and minds through Christ Jesus." There have been many men and women throughout time that were willing to face death at the hands of the wicked, all because of that peace supplied by our creator, and I hope I would be willing to do the same if faced with a similar situation.

As I drove home I wondered if Tim and Carmen had enjoyed themselves at the festival and after a service like we had that evening, I couldn't help but wonder if they had the same peace in their hearts that I have. The closer I got to home, the more this thought weighed on my mind, and I wondered if this might be the reason our paths had crossed.

I pulled into the driveway at fifteen minutes after nine, and noticed the two of them sitting on the front porch in the swing. After parking the car, I grabbed my Bible and headed out to greet them.

"Did you kids enjoy yourselves?" I asked, as I stepped onto the porch.

"Yes we did actually." Carmen answered, "I love looking at all the crafts and local artwork, and there's just something about the food when you're outdoors; it just tastes better for some reason."

Tim jumped in and said, "I don't know about the crafts, but the food was definitely the highlight of my evening."

"Sometimes I think food rates higher than me." Carmen said giving Tim one of those penetrating stares only a woman can give. "How about you Jack? How was your evening?"

"You kids missed out." I said, as I sat down in my rocker.

"We had a great service tonight; I think you would have enjoyed it, except for the fact that there was no food."

Tim laughed, knowing I had directed that remark at him.

"Sorry about that Tim, I couldn't help myself." I said, laughing with him.

"That's ok." He said, "I'm used to it; Carmen never lets me forget my love of food either."

"Well, I love food myself, and any time there's a meal after a service, believe me I'm there." I said, rubbing my stomach. "So tell me, do you kids have a home church in Mableton?"

"No." Carmen answered, "We don't really see a need for church."

I didn't expect that answer, but now I knew I was right about the purpose of our paths crossing, and now it was time for me to do my part for the Lord.

Chapter 2
No religion

"If you don't mind me asking, do you have something against churches?" I asked.

"Not churches per se, I just don't really believe in organized religion," Carmen explained. "I guess you could say I'm more of a *spiritual* person."

This is a phrase I've heard a lot in the past few years, so I asked, "What do you have against religion?"

"I just think it is man-made, and everyone seems to have their own very different version of it that they try to shove down everyone's throat."

"How about you Tim? What do you think?" I asked.

"I feel like maybe there's something out there greater than us, but there's no proof of its existence, so all we can do is have fun with the time we have and try not to hurt our fellow man in the process."

It was apparent to me by the looks on their faces that neither of them was concerned about Heaven or Hell, and I was going to have to work hard to help them.

"Carmen….when you say that you consider yourself to be a *spiritual being,* what does that mean exactly?"

Carmen tilted her head slightly, and looked toward the sky as she searched for a way to explain her belief. "Well I guess you could say….I feel like there is a force or something out there that makes things happen – I refer to it as God – I guess because that is a good name for it, but I think God is different for each individual person; we have to search within ourselves, and do what feels right for us, and in doing that, I feel like I connect *spiritually* with that entity."

I know that there are a lot of people in the world today who feel the same way Carmen felt, and it's due to the culture we live in. There are many people spreading this philosophy, and it is very easy to buy into, because it caters to our selfish natures, and creates a feeling of self-righteousness. In essence we all get to design our own god to fit whatever lifestyle we like to live. Unfortunately this is referred to in scripture as idolatry.

"It sounds like you've thought about this some." I said, as I studied her expressions.

"Yes." Carmen answered, "I think as intelligent beings, we can't help but think about it."

As human beings we tend to push our beliefs on other people when we are at odds with them – try to force them over to our way of thinking, but that generally puts people in a defensive mode, and ends up pushing them away instead, so I wanted to choose my words wisely. Many people, even though their intentions are good, end up coming across as over-bearing, and forceful, but Jesus teaches us to do things in a loving manner, because it will yield much better results. Proverbs 15:1 says, "A soft answer turneth away wrath: but grievous words stir up anger." It is much more profitable to approach people with meekness and love, than to belittle them by taking a strong-arm position against their beliefs.

"You are very right about that, and I myself can't imagine living without the knowledge there is a God out there in control. When you say you do what *feels* right to you, that's known as subjectivism; have you heard that term?" I asked, hoping she would be open to discussion.

"I've heard the term," she replied, "but no one has ever elaborated on it."

"Subjectivism is something taking place within an individual's mind, but unaffected by the outside world, in other words, different individuals will have different views about what feels right to them, because the reality going on in the outside world doesn't affect *their* view on things. It closely parallels something called relativism, meaning that everything is relative to each individuals perception." I could see a frown developing on her face. "Everyone tends to feel differently about many things – usually due to all the variables in each person's life, which happen to affect the way we look at things, and this is why no one needs to operate solely on *feelings*. One person may feel that violence and domination lead to peace, and another may feel that there is never a place for violence, and peace can only be achieved by diplomacy, so who's right? These two will always be fighting because their feelings are *subjective* instead of *objective.* You may feel that it's wrong to steal something from someone, but someone else may feel that they deserve what you have. Relativism leads to chaos not peace, and it's just an excuse to lead a life without accountability."

"I guess that would explain why so many people disagree on what's right." Tim stated.

"Yes," I said, with a cheerful laugh. "Without a common ground or foundation of truth, you end up with a lot of different *feelings* about what's true – there has to be a primmer, or focal point of *truth.* Relativism will teach that there is no absolute truth, but it is self-refuting because a person using this philosophy is making an absolute claim in order to say that there is no absolute truth. Fortunately we were created by a God who is involved with his creation and give us the standard. "

Tim looked at me as if he was about to hear some tired old story. "I guess your going to say the Bible is that primmer?" He said while rolling his eyes a little.

"Well, actually Jesus Christ is the truth, but the Bible is the revelation of that truth." I smiled as I gave that answer. "God gave us the scriptures so we wouldn't have to guess what's right and wrong; 2 Timothy 3:16-17 says, 'All scripture is given by inspiration of God, and is profitable for doctrine, for reproof, for correction, for instruction in righteousness: That the man of God may be perfect, thoroughly furnished unto all good works.' This basically states that the Bible is the supreme standard to live by, and it will teach us how to live. It's our owner's manual for life, and our road map to God, which never changes. Since we are creations of God and therefore accountable to him, it becomes extremely important to know what his position is on things. Our mere opinion is irrelevant and worthless if it disagrees with the one we're accountable to. In a court of law your feelings will not change the position of the law, and it's the same with God. There is a good reason why we need to focus on something that is unchanging, and that is simply because of the fallibility of human beings, which engenders the necessity of a common ground. Even with this common ground we can't rely on our ability to remember such an excessive amount of information, because very soon it would become totally distorted. This creates the need to continuously study its contents. How can we live a life pleasing to our creator, much less teach others to, if we are not referencing the creator's instructions? I remember doing an experiment in school once that consisted of lining 10 people up – shoulder to shoulder, and starting from one end, a secret phrase was whispered into the ear of one person, who was then told to pass it on to the next person in the same manner; this was repeated until the phrase was whispered into the final persons ear, and then they were asked to recite this phrase to the person who started the whole thing. Do you kids have any idea how that turned out?" I asked.

"I remember doing that same experiment in school myself," Carmen explained. "And by the time the story made it to the end, it was not the same as it was when it started."

"Exactly" I said. "This is why we must turn to God's Word as our source of truth, and not to human beings, or Hollywood's latest fad. When man tries to do it on his own things get distorted. That is why there are so many religions out there in complete disagreement with one another, and if you do some research on each one you'll find where many have had to be modified and manipulated in order to correspond with reality. Even then, a close study of these man-made religions will reveal erroneous and contradictory contents that would not be there if they were absolute truth."

It seemed that both Tim, and Carmen's natural response to scripture was to reject it by the looks on their faces, and the tone of their voices, but this doesn't come as a surprise to me, and it shouldn't to any Christian, because Satan promotes this type of outlook towards anything relating to God, especially if it challenges a persons presuppositions.

"There are a lot of different people out there saying a lot of different things about God, and the Bible, so I don't see how anyone can *know* they're right and others are wrong. What if all these different views and religions lead to the same God, or what if there is no God at all and people are just deceiving themselves?" Tim asked.

I knew I was going to have to dig deep to find the answers for these two, but I always enjoy helping people come to the knowledge of our Lord and Savior. I want others to feel the same joy I feel – the joy that comes with a relationship with God.

"That is a great question, Tim and I hope I can in some way prove to you that God is real, and the Bible is his word. I want to start by saying that it takes a measure of faith on everyone's part to find God, but it also takes faith to reject him and follow any of the many directions man's logic can take you. I myself am a Christian, and God has proven himself to me time and time again. The night when I was saved, that drawing power of God was unmistakably real, and once I put my faith and trust in Jesus Christ, the Holy Spirit changed my life from that point forward. All this was more proof than I could have ever asked for, unfortunately, I can't make anyone feel what I felt that night or even this day, in order to prove that the Holy Spirit is real, but I know that God can change a life. I say this, because I've been there, and let me tell you....when you get it right, you know it is right. There are many religions out there teaching all kinds of doctrines, and catering to any human emotion we can come up with, and when you say maybe all religions lead to the same God I have to disagree, because these different religions have tremendously different views about everything, and since we are all on the same journey, they can all be false, but they can't all be true. As I said a moment ago, study these other religions closely and you'll see the obvious problems with them. Now, as to whether or not there *is* a God, I'll say this; God has manifested himself to everyone in a general way. This is why man has always been searching for him, and as children before we are taught what to think and how to believe, we know in our hearts that there is a deity out there. Unfortunately we have the ability to suppress that knowledge and turn away from that search, or distort that search into a homemade religion that is worthless. Even with Christianity there has been distortion from the true teachings of Christ, but fortunately God has preserved his word. We have thousands and thousands of original manuscripts that we can turn to and make sure that our Bible has been translated properly, but even so, people still try to make their own way. There are many that parade around under the guise of Christianity, but contradict the teachings of Jesus Christ, which, are the teachings that Christianity is supposed to be based on. I'll explain some of these differences a little later if we have time, and you kids permit me to keep talking."

"If there is only one God, then there would have to be an absolute truth, and I just don't think absolute truth exists." Tim exclaimed.

"Well Tim, I'm going to do the very best I can to show you that absolute truth does exist, and that Jesus Christ is that truth – if you kids are willing to give an old man a chance." I said, hoping that they would at least hear me out.

"We'll definitely listen, but don't get your hopes up because I'm sure we've heard most of this before." Tim said, smiling in his confidence.

"That's fair." I said, "And besides, the things I'm going to say are based on facts that you may or may not be aware of, as well as, and most importantly God's word. In Isaiah 55:11 God says, 'So shall my word be that goeth forth out of my mouth: it shall not return unto me void, but it shall accomplish that which I please, and it shall prosper in the thing whereto I sent it.' So I am confident that his word will speak to you, and do what it is supposed to do when all is said and done, because after all the Bible is God's word."

I could see the skepticism on both their faces, but I could also tell that there was an eagerness to hear more – maybe test their loyalty to their beliefs, and try to prove them wrong.

"To answer your question about absolute truth Tim, we have to talk about what truth is." I recalled a story I once heard and decided it was relevant to this question. "Let's say Tim and Carmen, you're stopped by a state trooper for driving 85mph in a 55mph zone…he is likely to write you a speeding ticket, correct?"

"Yes" they both replied.

"What do you think his response will be if you say, "I *know* the speed limit is 85, so you can't write me a ticket; I sincerely believe it so it has to be true." "Do you think the law doesn't apply to you because your version of truth is different?" I asked knowing beforehand what the logical response would be.

"I wish it worked that way sometimes, but I know it doesn't." Carmen answered.

"That's right it doesn't" I replied. "That speed limit was previously set by the authorities, and even if a person ignores or misinterprets the postings, it will still stand as the limit. What's true is true no matter what we believe, or how sincere our belief is;

24

just because I may believe that tree in the front yard is a corn stalk, doesn't change the fact that it is a tree. This philosophy that each person has their own truth is nothing more than a manipulation of reality, and if embraced will ultimately lead to a breakdown of civilized society, because justice will no longer have a foundation. In most cases when someone refuses to accept the existence or authority of God as the truth, even in the midst of a plethora of evidence, it's because there is a sin or something in their lifestyle that would have to be given up in order to conform to God's plan, and they can't imagine giving it up. Instead they choose not to believe in the one true God, as if the lack of acknowledgement will force him to go away, or they will choose to design their own version of God – one that will permit the lifestyle they want to live. What they don't understand is that when you except Jesus Christ, and turn your life over to him, God gives us the Holy Spirit to make these changes possible. When a person is saved they no longer look at things the same way, and thus the things that once brought temporary pleasure will no longer possess the same appeal that once existed. There will always be temptation to fall back into these sins, but there will be a desire in your heart to keep God's commandments, and he promises to always give us a way out – we just have to take it. This leads to the question, how do we find out what's true about God?"

"I'm guessing your going to say the Bible." Carmen said sarcastically.

"Yes I am, but bear with me, and I think you'll see the validity of the Bible before we're done." I replied smiling again. "In John 4:24 it tells us that God is a spirit… now even though we can't see spirits, there are a multitude of people who believe there is a spiritual realm, even though some of them don't believe in God. Now just because we can't *see* God doesn't mean there is *no* God – gravity is real, but we can't see it, however, we can see the effects of it, so as a Christian I see the world, which is a big part of God's general revelation to all, and everything in it as an effect of God's creative power, and Psalm 19:1 says, 'The heavens declare the glory of God; and the firmament showeth his handiwork.' I think it's hard to take a close look at our world and not see it as a divine creation, and if this creator expects something from his creation, he would have to give us something to go by and that's where the Bible comes in, which is his special revelation, and it explains to an extent why things are the way they are, and most of all, what he expects of us. There are a multitude of verses that describe God as creator and the Bible is very clear that there is only one God that is responsible for this creation. One verse that references the existence of only one way to the one true God is John 14:6 where Jesus says, 'I am the way, the truth, and the life: no man cometh unto the Father, but by me.' Jesus stated very bluntly that he is *the way* not *one way* to the Father; then he goes on to say in John 6:44, 'No man can come to me, except the Father which hath sent me draw him: and I will raise him up at the last day.' which means that God will deal with your heart, and draw you to Jesus, but then it is up to you to respond to him, and put your faith and trust in him."

"I understand that the Bible teaches that, but how can we believe the Bible since man wrote it?" Tim interjected.

"2 Peter 1:20-21 says, 'Knowing this first, that no prophecy of the scripture is of any private interpretation. For the prophecy came not in old time by the will of man: but holy men of God spake as they were moved by the Holy Ghost.'" I answered. "And David was quoted in 2 Samuel 23:2 saying, 'The Spirit of the Lord spake by me, and his word was in my tongue.' This is another example of how the Holy Spirit works through us as human beings; he used these men to pen down exactly what he wanted them to write, without violating their natural abilities or writing styles. Even though there were approx. 40 different authors over a period of about 1500 years, you will notice that their writings are in perfect harmony but at the same time very different in style."

"I don't think you should use the Bible to prove the Bible." Carmen stated. "And how do we know Jesus is really the way, since he was human – maybe he was just a normal man who wanted to be a celebrity, or maybe he didn't exist at all." Carmen added.

I knew these questions would come up – they always do, and they're legitimate questions that all Christians should be prepared to answer, and if a question comes up that we don't know the answer to, we should try not to leave it unanswered, but always keep in mind that scripture is not concerned with answering every possible question our feeble minds can come up with. Sacrificing truth just to have an answer is not acceptable....we need to search the Bible for the answer or get help from someone more knowledgeable, but we should never ever make something up that just sounds good, because it will come back to haunt us, and maybe ruin our credibility with the person to whom we are witnessing. Sometimes we just have to say "I don't know" or "the Bible does not address that particular question."

"Well, I feel that it is important to show you what the Bible says, and I'm going to point out other evidences, in order to show you the Bible and reality are in harmony with one another. Since God is omnipotent and his word is unchanging, then it must always be true in relation to any aspect of reality it touches on; now that is not to say that it has to be scientifically precise on any area of science it addresses, but it must be true. As we go further I believe you will see that it is true, in every sense of the word, in relation to the world we live in. I guess the first thing we need to do now is determine whether or not there is a God, because there's no use talking about truth or the Bible, if there's no God responsible for inspiring it, and then we'll touch more on the Bible's legitimacy, and I'll tackle the questions about Jesus."

"Sounds good to me." Carmen replied.

"According to what you stated earlier, you both believe that the possibility exists for something greater than us out there, but you don't know what, and you see no proof correct?"

"I guess that about sums it up." Carmen answered.

I thought for a moment about the many directions I could go with this, and decided to go ahead and confront the inevitable question of how did we get here?

"The two biggest worldviews prevalent today are creationism, and evolutionism, even though there are many variations of each." I figured this would be a good place to start.

"Is there an eternal God who created the universe, or was there an enormous amount of eternal pre-existent matter condensed into a very small area that for some mysterious reason expanded in the big bang, which started the naturalistic process of evolution?" I asked. "Many evolutionists believe that the universe started with the big bang, which I'll get into later, and then through the process of evolving from non-living matter into single celled organisms – then continued to evolve into all the plants, animals, and human beings seen today. These two processes have one thing in common, and that is, there had to be a beginning. The laws of science state that for something to start to exist it must have a cause equal to or greater than itself, however, there inevitably has to be an eternal first cause. Creationists, along with some evolutionists, believe God is the *eternal first cause,* and most other evolutionists believe that matter must be eternal, even though they can't explain how non-living matter could change to living matter, then organize itself the way our universe is seen to be ordered. They are also unsure of why this massive expansion of space and time took place in the first place, as is the case for the *big bang* theory."

I could tell now that their interest was growing, because I'd mentioned the word *science.* Scientific evidence goes a long way with people, and contrary to popular belief, it undermines the *philosophy* not *science* of evolution.

"We'll start by explaining the evolutionary theory. There is a lot of confusion about what evolution actually is – there is a *fact* of evolution, which has truth to it, and a *theory* of evolution, which is the cause of many arguments."

"Are you about to say that you believe in evolution?" Carmen asked, with a very puzzled look on her face. Tim also had the "deer in the headlights" look about him.

"When it comes to truth I will stand by it, but theory is a whole other ball game. I'm going to try to clear up some confusion, and tell you what is true about evolution, and what is merely theory. I'm assuming that both of you have heard of DNA, genes, and the study of genetics." I said in a questioning manner.

Tim developed this mischievous smirk on his face then said "That's those building blocks they used to make dinosaurs in the movie Jurassic Park."

Carmen shook her head as she looked at me and said, "He bases a lot of his knowledge on movies, however, I think we are both familiar with the basics of genes and DNA." She said as she playfully smacked him on the arm.

I laughed at the obvious humor between them, "The genetic code is basically a set of blueprints used to build a living organism. Whatever is contained in these blueprints determines what kind of organism will develop, and then what features that organism will have. Evolution is a process involving the rearrangement, multiplication, and sometimes, mutation of genes, causing different variations within species over many generations. Another term for this is *micro-evolution*. This type of evolution has been observed and documented in laboratories for years and is evident in everyday life; let's take dogs for instance; there are many different breeds of dogs in this world, wild and domestic, which have evolved from the *original* pair of dogs; over time the genes varied, re-shuffled, and then throw in different breeding practices, and *wah-lah* we have the variety of dogs seen today. There are also adaptations built into the genes and chromosomes of animals, and humans that even allow us to *adapt* to our surroundings to some extent. These kinds of adaptations happen within *kinds,* and this is the evolution I agree with, and call fact, because it is proven and evident. I believe this is the way God wanted it, because without these changes within kinds, all of our pets would look alike, and so would we; we also wouldn't have the varieties of animals that we see today. I do wish, however, that people would use another term besides *evolving* because it causes people to automatically relate to the *theory*, not the *science*."

"Isn't that what Darwin was talking about?" Carmen asked.

"Not quite." I replied, "The Darwinian Evolutionary Theory is what's considered an *upward* or *progressive* evolution, and what that means is, over time as these genes change around and mutate, information in the genetic code is somehow increased to the point where you end up with a different, more sophisticated *species* - You may have heard this called *macro-evolution*."

"I guess this is how we descended from monkeys." Tim stated with his hands curled under his armpits in a feeble attempt to look like a chimp.

"Let's just say, this is the theory that started the whole, 'we evolved from chimpanzees' story. I'm also very happy to say that this form of evolution has never been fundamentally proven, and most scientists worth their salt will agree to that. Just like the example of dogs we talked about earlier, there is no known way to add genetic information, so the genetic variations are always in a *downward* or *regressive* direction, which means the original pair of dogs contained all the genetic information that is seen in every breed of dog today, but the dogs of today only carry part of the original information – and yet they are *still* dogs, and always will be because the genetic blueprint is that of a dog. Another point I would like to make is about the obvious differences between animals and human beings. God stated an obvious intentional difference between the two when he was describing creation; Genesis 1:24 says, 'And God said, Let the earth bring forth the living creature after his kind, cattle, and creeping thing, and beast of the earth after his kind: and it was so.' So basically he just said let it be and it was, but when he created man in verse 26 it says, 'And God said, Let us make man in our image, after our likeness: and let them have dominion over the fish of the sea, and over the fowl of the air, and over the cattle, and over all the earth, and over every creeping thing that creepeth upon the earth.' Then chapter 2 verse 7 says, 'And the Lord God formed man of the dust of the ground, and breathed into his nostrils the breath of life; and man became a living soul.' Do you notice the differences?"

Carmen was nodding her head. "There were three differences actually." She said. "Man was created in God's likeness, he was given dominion over the earth and animals, and he talked about the living soul."

"Very good." I said. "The creation of man was more precious than that of the animals – not to say our pets are not special to God and us, but we were created in his image and they were not. There has always been a difference in the purpose of animals as opposed to humans. We can all see these differences in everyday life; animals operate mainly on instinct and even though each has its own personality of sorts, they mainly go about doing whatever their instincts drive them to do. Humans on the other hand have a much more complex awareness of existence, and an internal need to seek out our purpose. People have contemplated their existence and purpose from the beginning of time, and throughout history the vast majority of men and women have believed in a supreme being, or in some cases *beings,* to go to for their answers. Biblical history teaches that the one true God of creation was taught from the beginning, but people tend to come up with their own versions that cater to their desires and so we end up with every type of belief system imaginable. Even though as time goes on people become more and more rebellious against their creator, there will always be many who seek God, unlike living instinctively as the animals do. Animals do what their creator programmed them to do, so they won't be out establishing their own animal church or religious sect. It all boils down to the fact that we as humans are programmed to seek God and glorify him, and they are not."

"I've never heard anyone explain it like that, but it makes sense; you don't see animals or people walking around in transient states. I don't think I've seen a dog starting to develop gills or wings wandering around town." Carmen stated with a look of enlightenment.

Tim couldn't resist jumping in himself, "You know, I wonder if the statement 'when pigs fly' is actually an assumption of the evolutionary process in the pork industry."

I couldn't help but laugh at his imagination. "It wouldn't surprise me Tim." I said, thinking to myself that someone out there probably believes that. "There *have* been genetic mutations that have to do with bodily functions observed in laboratories, but those mutations either reverted back to normal, caused some type of disability in the organism, or caused death; no mutation has led to an increase in information, and a more sophisticated organism, and therefore no *kind* of animal has ever changed into another *kind* of animal. If you really get into the study of genetics you will not believe how incredibly complex this genetic code is, and not only that but there is also the system that is responsible for reading the code and copying it. For some fish to be able to develop lungs and legs, and crawl up out of the ocean to walk on land is absurd."

The look on Tim's face was showing deep concentration as he obviously searched his mind for something, "You know; I heard someone defending evolution by referring to the flu virus, saying that it is evolving. What do you think about that?"

I remembered hearing that myself a while back. "This is exactly what I meant when I said we should use another term besides *evolving*. The flu virus is *adapting* and *changing*, which is an example of micro-evolution, but it is not a defense for the

Darwinian evolutionary process, because when all is said and done, it is still the *flu virus*. This is not limited to the flu either, because many other viruses adapt, and develop resistance to medications – and yet."

"They are still viruses." Tim finished my sentence for me.

"Yes they are Tim. The same can be said about bacteria as well. Bacteria are very interesting and can do some very interesting things, but it's because they have specialized genes that allow for these changes. In the end they are still bacteria."

"I see what you're saying," Tim stated, and looked as if the pieces of the puzzle were now fitting into their correct places. "What you say does make perfect sense. I guess there are many people, including myself, who don't really understand that there are different types of evolution, and not all types are in question."

"Exactly, Tim." I was so happy to hear him say that. "Because of this misunderstanding, there are those who use this as an opportunity to promote the theory under the guise of truth. They know that many people will be quick to defend the theory because they think they're defending true evolution."

Carmen stared at the floor for a moment, obviously thinking about all the opinions she had heard about evolution in the past, and then looked up at me with a genuine concern in her eyes.

"How could this have gotten so popular if there is no proof? I mean really, how can this be?" She asked.

I knew how she was feeling at that moment; it's like a feeling of betrayal, because we all want to trust the things we're taught in school, or see on the news, and it hurts to realize that we may have been misled.

"As I said, there are some who mix theory with true evolution in order to promote their agenda, and if a person doesn't study these things for his or herself it will be very easy to buy into with or without proof. I read a statement in a book once that hit the nail on the head… it said, 'The picture has become the proof.' That statement was referring to the pictures of ape-like creatures, gradually standing up and becoming human. There is no fossil evidence backing up these pictures; this is only an artist's rendering of someone's philosophy and opinion of life. Unfortunately, it is very easy for someone's opinion or theory to get a lot of publicity, especially if that someone is labeled *doctor* or *scientist*, because we automatically assume their credibility – now don't get me wrong, there are many credible doctors and scientists out there who *are* reliable, but some seem to get more media attention than others, all because of the *world view* of the ones giving the interviews. There are many interviews where Creation Scientists are defending creationism very thoroughly, but these interviews rarely ever make it to the public, because they don't fit in with popular belief."

"Why do you think they keep pushing this on us if there is no proof?" Tim asked.

"Well Tim, many people are willing to accept any explanation other than God and right now there is really only these two philosophies, in fact the goal of some is to turn people away from a belief in God, and no matter how lacking the evidence is for their explanations, they will continue to adjust things to fit their theory. They know that the general public will probably not take the time to research what they hear, and therefore indirectly promote things by word of mouth helping their cause. I also believe that there are some who are having trouble with their belief in evolution due to the conflicts and unanswered questions, but are worried about the trouble that will come their way if they suddenly change sides. I guess when you've staked a good portion of your life and reputation on something, it is very hard to admit that you may have been wrong, so they keep searching for something to save them. Colossians 2:8 says, 'Beware lest any man spoil you through philosophy and vain deceit, after the tradition of men, after the rudiments of the world, and not after Christ.' I'm going to give you kids something else to think about concerning proof; If upward evolution were true, there would be thousands, or maybe even millions of fossils out there of animals that were *in between* species, but we have an extensive fossil record that does not support molecules to man evolution – even Darwin realized that as the fossil record grew, a lack of transitional fossils would be devastating to his theory. They have found some deformed prehistoric animals, and some odd looking animals that have gone extinct without our awareness of their existence, but that's not unusual, it happens – in fact there should be animals and humans in the *in between* stages walking around now, but there are *not*."

Tim looked as if he were digging deep in his memory again for something, then perked up as he said, "I remember seeing an add on Google a while back that stated something about the missing link being found....was that a false add?" He asked.

"They continue to produce these so called missing links, but they end up being hoaxes, or mislabeled fossils, however, the missing link you're talking about was named Ida and they did try real hard to pass it off as the 'missing link', but it turns out Ida was just a fossil of a primate that very closely resembles a lemur. Chris Beard, who is curator of vertebrate paleontology at the Carnegie Museum of Natural History, stated: 'I actually don't think it's terribly close to the common ancestral line of monkeys, apes, and people....I would say it's about as far away as you can get from that line and still be a primate.' Now even though Mr. Beard included *people* in his ancestral line showing his belief in macro-evolution, even he doesn't consider it a missing link. I do want to say that there are many scientists out there who are searching for truth, and practicing true science, not hypothetical science, and these men and women deserve recognition for their efforts. I also know that assumptions have to be made at times, in order to get to the facts, but these assumptions don't need to be made public, because they are not proven, and once the different media outlets spread it around, it becomes fact to a lot of people – This in my opinion, discredits true science."

"I guess there are a lot of people like me who, because of our own laziness, or lack of concern, take what we hear or read in the news as fact, then pass it around to others without researching it first." Carmen said with an apologetic look.

"We have all been guilty of that at times," I said, "and we have to be careful not to spread rumors. Ecclesiastes 10:12 says: 'The words of a wise man's mouth are gracious; but the lips of a fool will swallow up himself.' Human beings do a lot of Satan's bidding for him with their mouths, whether they realize it or not. Did you know that when a snake bites something or someone, it can control just how much venom is released into the victim?" I asked, knowing they would both wonder what this had to do with our conversation, and by the looks on their faces I was right.

"That's a strange question to ask," Tim said confused. "But for what it's worth, I *have* heard that on the Discovery Channel, or maybe Animal Planet."

"Well, the reason I asked that is because we – just like the snake – can control how much damage we inflict just by controlling our tongues, which, is how humans release their venom."

Carmen looked at me with a big smile and said, "I have to give you credit Mr. Miller, you have definitely helped me realize what *true* evolution is – and how careful we need to be about our beliefs, but since you mentioned fossils, that brings up another question; what about dinosaurs, and frozen wooly mammoths? Isn't the Bible, and the pre-historic world in disagreement?" She asked.

"Evolutionists would love for us to believe that, but the Bible is in perfect agreement with our world today, *and* the pre-historic time period." I answered. "Have you kids ever heard of Ockham's Razor?"

"I don't think so." Carmen answered, and Tim agreed by shaking his head.

"Ockham's Razor come about from a 14th century logician, which is someone who studies the principles of reasoning, and it states: entities should not be multiplied unnecessarily, and everything being equal, the simplest explanation tends to be the correct one – the Bible just happens to be that simple explanation, and the world has had it for a very long time, even though many choose not to accept it."

"That's getting a little deep for my feeble mind, but I guess it makes sense." Tim said, looking confused.

We all laughed at his obvious humor.

"I'll go ahead and talk about the pre-historic topic, since it has come up, and it will begin the description of the creationist's point of view. The Bible shows our earth to be somewhere around six thousand years old, give or take, but many of the secular scientists say it's around 4.5 billion years old. The reason there is such a difference is, because secular scientists have to assume these extremely long periods of time in order for their theories to appear to work, but even then, they are in disagreement with each other due to all the flaws and unanswered questions that are created by these theories. I am going to take you through what God has said really happened and use these events to explain how things may have taken place many years ago, and you'll see that what the Bible says, and what we see around us are in total agreement. Are you kids ready for this adventure?"

"I actually can't wait to hear this." Carmen said as she leaned back making herself comfortable.

"I'm all ears." Tim stated.

"One thing we have to realize is that when we're talking about origins we're entering the realm of historical science, not empirical science, and no one can go back in time and see exactly how events unfolded, and we have to accept the fact that we may not ever be able to fully understand everything, because things in the present don't always explain the past, so all we can do is take the evidence available today, such as the Bible, historic records, fossils, and observation – and use them to the best of our knowledge to help with the pieces of the puzzle, and you will see that they are all in harmony with one another. If they are not complimentary someone will find it, because things won't add up, and this is exactly what has happened with the evolutionary point of view, and those who have taken the Bible out of context in order to make it seem contrary to reality. I also want you to be aware of the fact that the evidence being discussed and debated is the same for everyone. No one has different factual evidence; they just look at the evidence with very different presuppositions. Since we can't go back in time to know exactly what conditions on this earth were, an assumed starting point must be made, and that starting point will depend on our presuppositions. Another thing we should never do is assume we know what God is thinking, or the purpose behind anything he does. The information he wanted us to have is in the Bible, and this is what we must go by – adding to it or taking away from it makes it subjective instead of objective."

Tim held out his hand to stop me and said, "I think there are a lot of people who would say that science should replace the Bible when talking about evidence."

"I'm sure there are," I replied. "But the Bible *is* a historical document, as well as God's word, and what people have to realize is that science is always changing, and God's word remains constant, so the Bible, if true, should be in harmony with observation, but it and science will not always agree because of the changing scientific theories. Let me give you an example: The Egyptians in ancient days were a very intelligent race of people, but for many years they believed that the earth was held up by five pillars – the Greeks believed that Atlas held the earth on his shoulders, and there was also the belief that the earth was flat, but given enough time scientists will prove their theories wrong, and move on to another scientific theory, and of course today we know that the earth is suspended in space, because space travel has given us a birds eye view."

I turned in my Bible to the book of Job and said, "The original Bible manuscripts have been around for thousands of years, and evidence of God's inspiration is shown here in Job 26:7 which says, 'He stretcheth out the north over the empty place, and hangeth the earth upon nothing.' How do you think Job would have known that the earth was held up by nothing way before space travel was able to prove it?"

I could see that Carmen and Tim were in deep consideration of this question, because of the intensity of their expressions.

"Another example can be found in Isaiah 40:21, 22 which states, 'Have ye not known? Have ye not heard? Hath it not been told you from the beginning? Have ye not understood from the foundations of the earth? It is he that sitteth upon the circle of the earth, and the inhabitants thereof are as grasshoppers; that stretcheth out the heavens as a curtain, and spreadeth them out as a tent to dwell in:' this describes the earth as a circle, even though many scientific minds chose not to accept it until many centuries later. There were Greek and Muslim scholars in the eighth and ninth centuries who, through mathematical equations, had shown the earth to be a sphere, but not all believed. Some expected Christopher Columbus to sail off the edge of the earth, but of course he didn't. Again this information has been available for a very, very, very long time."

"That is *very* interesting indeed." Carmen stated.

"I'm sure you two have heard of oceanography, and ocean currents haven't you?"

They both nodded their heads.

"There is even a reference to ocean currents in Psalm 8:8, which calls them paths of the seas. Oceanographers didn't discover these hidden currents until our recent past – many years after it was written about in the Psalms. These are just tiny examples of the evidences of inspiration in the Bible. Science stems from the fallible knowledge of man, and this is why it is volatile. Throughout history you can watch as scientific theories have evolved into new and different theories, you may even be familiar with claims made by scientists in our recent past that black holes were non- existent, but now they're on the air telling us otherwise. I look at science as reverse engineering. God created the universe – he designed it – he knows how all the intricate parts work together – and only he knows all the correct answers. Scientist's are taking the finished product – taking it apart as much as they can – and trying to get back to the beginning, which is not a bad thing by no means, but theories should not be presented as truth. I don't want this to sound like absolute science bashing, but I do want you to understand that even though science can answer questions at times, it is also very vulnerable, because it is ever changing, and who knows, maybe one day it will catch up with the Bible."

We all laughed, and I couldn't help but think about how much truth was in that statement, even if they didn't realize it.

"I know we got a little off track there so I'll continue on with the pre-historic topic if you kids are ready."

"By all means" Carmen said cheerfully.

"Lets see, now where was I? – Oh yes, I'm going to show you how the Bible is complementary to the prehistoric world, dinosaurs, wooly mammoths, and the ever popular ice age. There are approximately 60 different theories, depending on who you ask, encompassing ice ages and the extinction of dinosaurs and wooly mammoths. Each are filled with holes, and each solution they come up with leads to more questions. There is an astonishing amount of information out there about the ice age and these giants of our past, and some of it gets pretty in depth so I'm going to just touch the surface of these topics; I'll be glad to point you in the direction of some great books if you want to go deeper."

Carmen was smiling intently, because this conversation was apparently catering to her intellectual side, but Tim still looked as if he was searching for faults in everything I said. I decided to make sure that I hadn't left anything too open with him so I asked. "Has everything I've said made sense, and answered your questions thoroughly so far Tim?"

"Yes." He answered, "I just have so many questions, and it's hard to put them in order."

"Fair enough." I said. "I'll try to bring things up in an order that works for everyone, but if you think of something in the mean time, don't hesitate to ask ok."

"Deal" Tim said.

I opened my Bible to the book of Genesis. "We know that dinosaurs and wooly mammoths existed, because we see the evidence in our fossil record; Genesis 1:24, which, is describing the sixth day of creation says, 'And God said, let the earth bring forth the living creature after his kind, cattle, and creeping thing, and beast of the earth after his kind: and it was so.' This means that animals, including dinosaurs and wooly mammoths were created on the sixth day; verse 26 says 'And God said, let us make man in our image, after our likeness: and let them have dominion over the fish of the sea, and over the fowl of the air, and over the cattle, and over all the earth, and over every creeping thing that creepeth upon the earth.' This means man was created on the same day, so man and dinosaurs lived at the same time, unlike the alternative theory which states that we did not exist together."

Carmen had an inquisitive look about her as she asked, "Is there proof that both lived at the same time?"

"There is actually quite a bit of proof, even though evolutionists tend to ignore it. A majority of fossils are found in the cretaceous rock layer, which evolutionists say was formed millions of years before man came into being. The funny thing is that male and female footprints and handprints have been found along side, and crossing dinosaur footprints in this very rock layer, along with fossil remains. Spear marks have been found on the bones of some of these fossils, which show that man was hunting these animals. You can look up photos of some of these prints by checking out the Paluxy riverbed located in Texas. Bones from a human hand were also found in this same riverbed, but don't think this is the only evidence found. These evidences have been found not only in the U.S. but also in South Africa, and other locations around the world. They even have a petrified human finger that was found in this cretaceous rock layer, which, even though evolutionists refute it, cat-scans show that it is no hoax. There are a lot of arguments back and forth about these findings, and sometimes it's hard to determine whether or not evidence has been tampered with, but it's up to us as individuals to look at both sides of the story and try to sort out fact from theory. These examples relate to the fossil record, but there are other examples that relate to historic findings. Ancient Aztec burial stones have drawings of dinosaurs on them – cave paintings of dinosaurs have been found in Europe – ancient figurines of dinosaurs are on display in China, and even Native American weavings have depictions of dinosaurs on them. These drawings just didn't appear on their own, and they're too harmonious with what we know to be true, and with other ancient depictions, to be from so many different people's imaginations, so I would say the answer to your question is yes." I stated.

"I guess they don't divulge that information easily." She said with disgust. "One more question before you go on – What if the days spoken about in the Bible are on a different time scale than what we're used to; what if those days were actually thousands or millions of years in Gods eyes, which, would go along with the scientists theories?"

"That is a very good question." I responded smiling, "But God thought about that when these scriptures were written, and if you'll notice in verses 5, 8, 13, 19, 23, and 31 of Genesis chapter 1, God ended each day by saying, 'and the evening and the morning were the first day.' and this was repeated for each subsequent day. His reference to the evening and morning gives us no reason to think they were more than a normal 24 hour day. Also keep in mind that if there were millions of years of evolution before man, then that would mean death before sin, and that's not what the Bible teaches."

"You know I've heard that a thousand times in Sunday school as a kid, but it never registered to me how these little details are embedded in the verses." Tim said, nodding his head with a look of enlightenment.

"Believe me Tim, I have missed a lot through the years myself." I said in agreement. "But we must pay attention to details, because as we see in Mathew 5:18 Jesus said, 'For verily I say unto you, Till heaven and earth pass, one jot or tittle shall in no wise pass from the law, till all be full-filled.' The words *jot* and *tittle* refer to the smallest letter and mark in the Hebrew alphabet, and signifies the importance of these tiny details."

"I'll have to take your word for the Hebrew alphabet reference," Carmen said. "Because I have no understanding of the Hebrew language."

"I can't speak or read Hebrew either," I added. "But there are references in my study Bible that help me understand some of the translations, and it comes in very handy, so if I say some word that makes no sense, stop me and I'll elaborate. One thing that needs to be mentioned is that the name dinosaur wasn't invented until sometime in the 1800's, which is why you won't see that word in the Bible or in documents originating before this time period, but in Job 40:15-18 the Lord is telling Job 'Behold now Behemoth, which I made with thee; he eateth grass as an ox. Lo now, his strength is in his loins, and his force is in the navel of his belly. He moveth his tail like a cedar: the sinews of his stones are wrapped together. His bones are as strong pieces of brass; his bones are like bars of iron.' The word behemoth is referring to a very large animal, and this animal eats grass, has bones like iron bars, and has a tail like a cedar tree, which, to me sounds an awful lot like a dinosaur in the herbivorous category. There are other descriptions of these animals referred to as *dragons,* and even a great sea creature named Leviathan is mentioned in the Bible. This is not restricted to the Bible alone either; there are many ancient writings that are not Biblical, but also describe dragons and monsters, which fit the mold of dinosaurs very well; Fictional writings and Hollywood have turned dragons into a mythical creature, but they very well could have been dinosaurs in disguise. Evolutionists will tell you that dinosaurs ruled the earth 140 million years, and went extinct about 65 million years ago, without the presence of man, but they are wrong on both accounts. The Bible says that we were created at the same time, and if you trace back the genealogy of the Bible, it will show that all this happened about six thousand years ago, not millions of years."

"Where did they come up with millions of years?" Carmen asked.

"When someone digs up a fossil, they use different types of dating systems to give a scientific guess as to how old the object in question is; these are questionable because of assumptions and inconsistencies, but because it is impossible to know for sure how old something is without knowing every possible thing - climatic and otherwise - that could have effected it since it was buried, these assumptions have to be taken lightly – for instance, when there is volcanic activity, the gases mix with precipitation and create sulfuric acid – also known as acid rain, which has a negative effect on rocks, sediments, and anything that comes into contact with it, causing them to appear older than they are. The reason they use millions and billions of years in their theories is, because they need this amount of time to make their theories seem like they could actually work. We also have to be inquisitive about the questions that were asked in order to come up with these dates, and you will find that when a different approach to the evidence is taken, there is also a very different answer."

"Can you defend your criticism of these dating methods?" Tim asked. "I was under the assumption that dating methods are a reliable proof of the age of the earth."

"Well Tim, it all comes down to assumptions. Let's just pick one very popular dating method, and use it as an example of how inaccurate it can be. Carbon-14 dating is very well known and widely used so we'll discuss this one to begin with. Carbon-12 and Carbon-14 are created in our atmosphere and are taken in by every living organism, and there is a consistent ratio of Carbon-12 to Carbon-14 atoms that can be measured. At the time of death, this ratio begins to change because Carbon-14 is an unstable atom unlike Carbon-12, which is stable. This means that Carbon-14 is always decaying, and since the organism is dead, there will be no more taken in to replace that which is going away. Scientists know how long it takes for this decay to take place, which is measured in half-life's, so they can use the ratio of Carbon-12 to the remaining Carbon-14 found in a specimen to determine how long it has been dead. This measurement is actually very accurate, but the problem is with the ratio; you see, the ratio in any organism will always be consistent with the ratio that is present in our atmosphere at the time of death. Scientists are assuming that the atmosphere has always been the same as it is today, but the Bible and other evidences show that the world has gone through some serious changes in the past, and our atmosphere would have been very different a few thousand years ago. If the atmosphere was different, then we no longer have an accurate starting point, and therefore cannot determine the correct ratio of anything that died previous to the recording of atmospheric measurements."

"Wow!" Tim exclaimed. "I sort of expected to stump you on that one, but I'm impressed. How do you know this stuff?"

"Well Tim, as I said, it's up to us to research these things and I wanted to know where their dates were coming from. After doing a lot of searching, I learned quite a bit about why you get a different answer from different people when it comes to the age of a particular specimen. Different labs will give different ages of the same specimen all because of presuppositions. This also applies to radioisotope dating methods, which are used on non-organic specimens like rocks, and unfortunately it all goes back to the assumed starting point which cannot be known for certain, and no one can guarantee that there was no contamination of a specimen over the many years it has lain in an open environment.

Carmen was nodding her head in agreement, which was a good sign, because it meant that I wasn't confusing them too bad. Sometimes I get a little over zealous and bounce around too much.

"So even if the ages are wrong, we are still talking about an extinct species; does the Bible say what happened to them?" Tim asked.

"Are you familiar with the story of Noah's Ark?" I asked.

"Yes." They both answered.

"Well after Adam and Eve's rebellion against God, life changed on earth, and God punished sin with the curse of death; this in my opinion would have been the start of the atmospheric changes I mentioned a moment ago. Later on sin got so bad that God described the world – animals included – as *wicked* and instructed Noah to build the Ark. In Genesis chapters six and seven, God tells Noah to fill the Ark with two of every kind of animal, and seven of some, which would have included dinosaurs, and wooly mammoths."

Tim held out his hand to stop me for a second and said, "I've never understood how all these animals could fit on one boat?"

I paused for a second to recall some things I had read about this and answered, "Well, this *boat* was very large – according to the measurements listed in the Bible, it had about 95,700 square feet of deck space, and it didn't say that all these animals were full grown; they could have all been younger, and much smaller animals, so it would have held them without a problem; you also have to realize that all things are possible for an entity that can create a universe." I said smiling. "Plus remember how I talked about variations within kinds of animals a little earlier."

They both nodded their heads.

"That means only the original pairs were on the Ark, and the many varieties we have today have come about since then, so I believe there would have been plenty of room."

"If they were on the Ark then your saying they survived the flood." Carmen stated questioningly.

"Yes, this would mean that every species of animal on the Ark survived – and speaking of the flood, I believe this would have been the next cataclysmic event that would have wreaked havoc on our atmosphere. When all this water started raging over the earth, all the land animals, and sea creatures perished along with every human being except those on the ark; many were buried in tombs of mud and silt, which preserved them as the fossils we see today. You see in order for an organism to become fossilized it has to be buried quickly upon its death to protect it, otherwise scavengers will consume and drag pieces of it all over the place, and decay quickly sets in preventing it from being preserved. Fossilization is very problematic for the evolutionist's because they do not accept the flood as truth, and believe that all these fossils we have were laid down gradually over time as creatures died and then were covered with the natural accumulation of sediment. They also believed at one time, that it took a long time for something to fossilize, but now even they admit that if chemical composition is correct, fossils can form in a matter of hours, days, or weeks. If you want to go a little deeper into this subject, it may interest you to read about the soft tissue that has been discovered in many dinosaur fossils; soft tissue should not exist in something that is 65 million years old or older." I said, hoping they both would embark on this journey.

"How could sedimentation possibly work?" Carmen asked. "If animals have to be buried quickly to be fossilized, sedimentation is not a viable answer."

"Bingo!" I exclaimed. "Sedimentation is a very slow process, and there is no way these carcasses would last long enough for fossilization to take place, so you'll hear many scientist claim localized flooding was the cause. Another clue as to how it actually happened can be found when one observes these fossil beds. A very high number of fossils are found in mass graves; since animals don't bury each other, it would only make sense that these large numbers of animals were trapped and buried by some catastrophe."

"That sounds logical." She replied. "When you think about animals that die in the wild, or are hit by cars, their bodies are soon torn apart and disappear. They also don't tend to die all in one place."

"I couldn't have said it better myself" I smiled. "The great flood can also answer the ice age questions, which I'll get into in a moment, and the flooding and receding of massive amounts of water also explain the different rock layers and canyons we see in the world, because if you've ever seen the effects of even a small flood, you know just how much it can change the landscape."

"It can definitely make a mess, but do you really think it created giant canyons?" Tim asked.

"Oh yes." I replied. "You have to keep in mind that the whole earth was covered completely with water, and I know it's hard to comprehend, but there would have been massive amounts of localized floods, and landslides occurring constantly as the water was building up to its maximum level, but when this water started to recede….that's when much of the carving would have taken place. If you look at what's called the 'lay of the land' you will normally be able to see the path that water would travel when given the chance to drain, because it naturally runs downhill, and when you funnel an amount of water such as was present during the great flood down these natural run-offs, it would do some serious carving, and because these are natural drainage areas, you will notice that most of them still have water running in them today. Scientist's look at time frames for the erosion process under normal climatic conditions, which is why they say it has taken millions of years to create these canyons, but if you consider a global floods impact, the process can then been downsized to days or months give or take. We also have observable evidence of very large canyons and wastelands being created in a matter of days as the result of water erosion after volcanic activity. Since we're on the subject of the flood, I'll just go through the whole story, and end with the extinction of these many animals."

"Sounds good." Tim said.

"Noah was the only one who found grace in the eyes of the Lord during this *wicked* time period, so he and his wife, and his three sons, and their wives were to be saved with the building of the Ark – Genesis 7:11 says, 'In the six hundredth year of Noah's life, in the second month, the seventeenth day of the month, the same day were all the fountains of the great deep broken up, and the windows of heaven were opened.' This is when the rain started falling, and water sources from the great deep opened up; some speculate that giant cracks in the earths crust opened up, releasing subterranean water, and also initiating extreme volcanic activity, which geologists have verified. It has also been speculated that before the flood the earth was surrounded by a giant vapor canopy which would have given the whole earth a more tropical climate because of the greenhouse effect. I don't know if that is true or not but it could be because the Bible clearly states that it had not rained before this time, and this type of an atmosphere would explain why Carbon-14 dating shows organisms to be many, many thousands of years old. The book of Genesis says it rained for forty days and forty nights, in addition to the water coming from the fountains of the great deep, allowing the water to rise to fifteen cubits, or approximately twenty two and a half feet above the highest peak. The earth would have been in complete turmoil at this time, and geologists have uncovered evidence of deep water all over the world, even in places like the Sahara desert, along with, evidences of extreme volcanic activity by observing interlaced layers of lava flows, and volcanic ash. Now if my memory serves me correctly, the duration of the flood and its receding was about three hundred and seventy one days, and then the Ark rested on the mountains of Ararat seventy four days after the water started receding."

"You know," Carmen interjected. "When you describe it like that, it becomes more real. I guess it never registered to me just how big a global flood actually would be, and how much devastation would inevitably follow."

"It is hard to understand." I said, "Since we've never seen anything even come close to a disaster of this magnitude, but if you watch the news you can see many smaller floods, mudslides, and volcanic activity happening all over the world, and it gives us a small taste of what it would have been like back then."

"What about the ice age?" Tim asked. "How could a flood cause that?"

"Well, as I said before, this can get very deep so I'm just going to scratch the surface. The reason people bring up wooly mammoths and the ice age is, because the Bible doesn't specifically mention them, so they assume that it must be wrong. I'm going to give you something to think about, and you can research it for yourselves at your leisure. Now keep in mind that, as I said before, no one can go back in time and see exactly how events unfolded, but I want you to see that there is a very possible Biblical explanation that you won't see on the 6'oclock news, or hear about in school. There are all sorts of evidences that show an ice age happened. A couple of examples include striated rocks marked by the glaciers as they moved through areas that today have a very tolerable, even pleasant climate, and contrary to popular belief, these marks support a young earth because of the small amount of erosion that has taken place since, and another example would be moraines, or mounds of debris pushed and piled up by these giant glaciers. I don't think anyone is arguing against the occurrence of an ice age, but discussion of time frame and the number of ice ages does invite controversy. We also know that mammoths and many other animal fossils have been found all over the world, but the ones that get the most publicity are the ones found in Siberia. Siberia today is an extremely cold climate, and many fossils have been found frozen in the permafrost layer – some with skin, hair, internal organs – some in standing or sitting positions, and some with food still in their stomachs. They have also been found with trees and bushes buried with them, and some were found to have died from suffocation. You may have even heard of some with flesh that is fresh enough to eat, but that seems to be a big myth."

"What exactly is permafrost?" Tim asked.

"Well as I said before, Siberia is an extremely cold place today, and the ground is permanently frozen sometimes hundreds of feet deep, and even in the summer months, only a couple of feet will thaw, so basically it's permanently frozen."

"I think I read something once about animals being flash frozen during the ice age." Carmen said, while trying to remember where. "Do you think that's what really happened?"

"I'm sure you have seen that since this is what many scientists believe happened, but there was a study done to determine how cold it would have to be to flash freeze an animal this size, and they came up with an astonishing negative 150 degrees Fahrenheit – the problem is that there are approximately sixty different theories as to how this ice age scenario could happen, and they have been picked apart, because of errors and inconsistencies with reality. It would take a major geological event to trigger an ice age because of its complexity, and scientists have a hard time finding something that thoroughly explains all of these findings, because they will not accept the flood, but I'm happy to say that the great flood could have caused all of this. Our ocean temperatures and currents have a lot to do with our weather, so what do you think would happen if the whole world all the sudden became one big ocean?" I asked.

"It would probably be a weather forecasting nightmare." Tim said laughing.

"I believe you're right about that Tim." I replied. "There are two major components needed for an ice age – very cold and constant temperatures, and a lot of moisture to fuel ongoing snowfall with very little melting; the problem is that it is very difficult to maintain a scenario like this naturally without a major geologic driving force. With the earth flooded, the climate would have been in an uproar, and the extreme volcanic activity that has been discovered, would have launched unbelievable amounts of ash and gasses into the atmosphere, which as we know from Mt. St. Helen, and other volcanoes, causes the sunlight to be reflected back into space, and leads to a drop in the temperature of all related areas. The ash cloud from a single volcano has been known to drop the temperature over the entire earth about three degrees for at least two years, so you can imagine what constant volcanic activity all over the world could do. Temperatures would drop causing ice to form, which would add to the reflection of sunlight and therefore causing even more radiant heat loss. There would also be elevated amounts of evaporation to fuel the snowfall caused by a much larger surface area of water, which would have probably been very warm since much of it came from below the earths crust, and amazingly enough, you have the start of an ice age. I really do encourage you to pick up a book about this, because there is a lot more detail than I can go into."

"I guess I can follow that." Carmen stated, "But where does that leave Noah and all the animals?" she asked.

"You have to remember that only certain parts of the earth were covered in ice: maybe somewhere in the neighborhood of 30 percent of our land masses. After the ark came to rest, Noah and his family lived in the middle-east around the Euphrates, and Tigris rivers for somewhere between one hundred and three hundred years until the Tower of Babel incident."

"What was the Tower of Babel incident?" Tim asked.

"Well, in Genesis 9:1 it states, 'And God blessed Noah and his sons, and said unto them, be fruitful, and multiply, and replenish the earth.' But instead of replenishing the earth, they all stayed together in one area, and Genesis chapter eleven describes how they decided to build a city, and a tower that reached to Heaven in pursuit of making a name for themselves. It is also believed that this tower served a purpose in the worship of false god's as well. In order to put a stop to this tower, and replenish the earth Genesis 11:7-9 says, 'Go to, let us go down, and there confound their language, that they may not understand one another's speech. So the Lord scattered them abroad from thence upon the face of all the earth: and they left off to build the city. Therefore is the name of it called Babel; because the Lord did there confound the language of all the earth: and from thence did the Lord scatter them abroad upon the face of all the earth.' So this was God's response to their rebellion."

"Ok." Tim said nodding his head, "That actually answers another question that I had about how all the different cultures and races of people came about."

"It's all about the details." I said smiling, and I couldn't help but think about how revealing God's word is if we just pay attention to the details. "All these different groups of people created isolated gene pools, and each group developing different adaptations to their environment – passing down traits to their offspring – would allow for different variations in appearances to be passed down from generation to generation."

"I've always heard the saying that, 'we all came from Adam and Eve.' But I never wondered about why there are so many different languages, and appearances." Carmen said amazed.

"It's easy to overlook these things, but the answers are there if we choose to look for them, and accept them." I said. "Now to continue on with the story…. after all this happened, man and animals alike were greatly multiplying in large numbers, and all were able to migrate around the world through all the ice free areas, and even Siberia was a very habitable place at this time; the food in the stomachs of the mammoths was vegetation, and fossils of ferrets and ground squirrels, which are burrowers, show that this area was a grassland during the ice age. It has been speculated that before the flood our land area was a super continent named Pangaea, meaning one large continent. The Bible also implies this in Genesis 1:9-10 where it states, 'And God said, Let the waters under the heaven be gathered together unto one place, and let the dry land appear: and it was so. And God called the dry land Earth; and the gathering together of the waters called he Seas: and God saw that it was good.' This does sound like the possibility of a single land mass to me. After the breaking apart of the super continent caused by plate tectonics, there may have been more movement of animals and people across things known as land bridges which allowed access between the newly separated continents."

"I'm guessing plate tectonics is referring to the movement of the massive plates that float on the molten sea underneath us." Carmen stated inquisitively.

"Yes it is, and these plates still move today." I reassured. "Just not as fast."

"Another interesting thing that is found in these same areas is the fossils of early man. I'm sure you've both heard of cavemen haven't you?"

"Oh yes." Carmen said, and Tim nodded in agreement.

"Science refers to them as Neanderthals or Cro-Magnon men, and their remains have been found in the same areas as the mammoths. They're called cavemen, because the evidence found in caves such as drawings and tools show that they were living there." I said, "And even though some want to call them missing links, because of their bone structure, and facial features, they are almost identical to man today. These differences can be explained by diseases they were known to have, and interbreeding. Now to answer your question about what happened to all these animals, there are many theories about this, but what makes the most sense to me is that as the ash and gases dissipated from the atmosphere, the climate started the process of balancing itself, and returning to normal – the ice began to melt, and more floods occurred causing more mudslides, which would entomb trees and animals in all sorts of positions. Some animals would be trapped in areas such as Siberia, where the climate was taking a turn for the worst, and those entombed in the mud and silt would be consumed by the developing permafrost as temperatures began to plummet. Since the main digestive process of mammoths occurs in the intestines, their stomach contents would be somewhat preserved long enough for them to freeze."

"Why were mammoths the only animals that seem to have been affected by all this?" Carmen asked.

"Actually they weren't." I answered. "There were many different kinds of animals that went extinct during all this, which, is evident in our fossil record, but it didn't all happen at one time; some survived the localized floods and the entrapment, but ended up dying in the massive dust storms that came about during the climate change as hot and cold temperatures mixed, and the earth began searching for normal."

"I have never heard anything about dust storms." Tim stated in disbelief.

"There was actually a dust storm in the mid-western United States back in the 1930's that partially buried houses and barns, so it would be easy for one to bury an animal caught in the storm, and that would explain the mammoths that were found to have died of suffocation just as others were suffocated by entrapment in the mudslides."

"I think I remember something about that; they called it the great dust bowl or something." Carmen added.

"I'm not sure about the name it was given, but you could be right." I replied, "This would explain many of the deaths suffered by all these animals, and the rest can be explained by simple extinction. Animals go extinct all the time, and for different reasons – it could have been climate, competition for food, disease, or maybe some were even hunted to extinction by man. There's even the possibility that some survived in very remote areas of the world, and are alive today – who knows? If scientists can discover new species they didn't know existed, then why not one that was thought to be extinct? It has happened; I read just the other day that a spider has been found, which was thought to be extinct since none had been observed in over 30 years, but this is a prime example of the possible outcome of assumptions."

"You seem to have an answer for everything Jack." Tim stated.

"Actually the Bible has the answers God deems necessary, we just have to look them up." I answered. "And again I recommend that you do some more research on the ice age, because I have left out a lot of the evidences that have been found."

"You've got my curiosity up, so I think I *will* do some reading on this subject." Carmen replied.

"Now back to how the world came to be, you were about to tell us the creationists viewpoint as opposed to the evolutionary theory, before we got you sidetracked." Tim reminded, "Since evolution doesn't explain the way things are, what do creationists have to offer?"

I glanced down at my watch and realized it was very late so I decided to post-pone the next topic until the next day. "How about we continue this in the morning?" I asked with a yawn. "I just realized its 3 o'clock in the morning and this old man can't stay up all night like I used to."

"I can't believe it's this late already." Carmen said surprised.

"That's a good thing though, because it means the conversation was so good that time flew."

Tim and I both laughed and nodded our heads in agreement as we all got to our feet and started in the house.

"You kids make yourself at home, and try to get some good sleep; if you need anything I'll be right down the hall." I said as I locked the front door and turned out the porch lights. They went into their room, and I went to mine with a very happy feeling inside, which always seems to accompany glorifying the Lord. I was so happy to have the chance to defend Christianity against the evil of this world, and it was good knowing that the Conley's were open minded enough to at the least listen to what I had to say.

As I layed in bed I closed my eyes and prayed, asking God to give me the words to say to them, so that the seed would be planted in their hearts, allowing God to deal with them in his own way, and help them realize their need for a savior.

Chapter 3
Creationism

I awoke Thursday morning as the sunlight began peeking through the small spaces between the blinds and window frames, making its way onto my face. After a few minutes of stretching, and going through the process of waking up, I made my way into the bathroom, and started the daily routine of getting cleaned up and presentable. After dressing, I walked out into the hallway and noticed the door to their room was already open and the bed was made up. My first thought was that maybe I had offended them with something I'd said the night before, and they had decided to leave before I got up, but then I noticed the grandfather clock by the window, which was about to chime for the eleven o'clock hour, and I couldn't believe I had slept that long. As I walked into the living room I could hear their voices coming from outside so I meandered out to greet them.

"Good morning." I said as the screen door closed behind me.

"Good morning." They both repeated.

"Have you kids been up long?" I asked. "I don't normally sleep this long; I must have been very tired."

"We've been up for a couple of hours," Carmen answered. "and just got back from the coffee shop downtown. We brought you back a regular coffee since we didn't know what you liked." She said as she handed me the still steaming cup.

"Thank you very much." I said gratefully. "I'll drink almost anything, so regular coffee is just fine, and very much needed right now.

"It's our fault; we kept you up too late last night." Tim said apologetically.

"Oh, that's ok, I really enjoyed the conversation, and I think it was worth staying up for." I said while trying to get the caffeine in me as quick as possible.

"We normally sleep longer than we did, but I think we were both looking forward to continuing our discussion, which made it hard to stay in bed longer than necessary." Carmen said with noticeable excitement on her face.

"Did ya'll eat while you were out?" I asked.

"No." Tim replied. "But I think it's about time."

"I'm sure *you are* famished." I said, smiling at Tim. "So why don't we head back into town and have an early lunch, and we will continue our talk." I suggested.

"Sounds good to me." Carmen replied.

"You don't have to ask me twice." Tim added.

We walked down to a little café on the edge of town that Shirley and I used to visit from time to time; their food has always been good, and the service even better.

"Will this be alright for you kids?" I asked, "Or should we look for something else?"

"This is fine with me." Tim replied.

"We saw this place yesterday," Carmen added, "and we talked about trying it out before we left town."

We sat down to a nice leisurely lunch – I had a chicken salad sandwich, which I love –they both ordered roast beef sandwiches, and judging by how quick they disappeared, I think they rather enjoyed them as well.

"I really am sorry we kept you up so late last night." Carmen explained, "But we really did enjoy our talk, and I am very anxious to hear what else you have to say."

"Oh, that was no problem at all, I really enjoyed it too, and I really appreciate you kids being willing to listen to another point of view, but after this is all over, I strongly urge you to study the Bible for yourselves, and not just take my word for it, or anyone's word for that matter. There are false teachers out there in all kinds of disguises, even though God's word is clear about how he feels about it. Revelation 22:18-19 says, 'For I testify unto every man that heareth the words of the prophecy of this book, If any man shall add unto these things, God shall add unto him the plagues that are written in this book: And if any man shall take away from the words of the book of this prophecy, God shall take away his part out of the book of life, and out of the holy city, and from the things which are written in this book.' Now, I don't know about you, but I don't think I want to get on God's bad side"

"That did sound pretty serious." Tim stated, "But I still think we have a little way to go before I'm completely convinced."

"I do appreciate your honesty Tim, and all I ask from you is that you think about what is said, and if God starts dealing with your heart, it is then up to you to have faith in him and repent from your sins, but I never want you to think that I'm trying to force anything down either one of your throats."

Carmen dropped her head for a moment, "I'm sorry I said it that way yesterday, because you have definitely been anything but forceful, and I really appreciate that."

"Don't feel bad about that," I said, hoping she didn't think I had taken offence to her original remarks. "You answered my question with honesty, and apparently someone has been forceful with you in the past, or you wouldn't have said that; you didn't offend me in the least, and I hope I can – if anything – break the stereotype."

"You've already done that." She said, and I noticed Tim nodding his head in agreement.

"Do you kids want to check out the festival today? Or is there something else you'd rather do?"

"Actually, I'd like to head back to your front porch, and continue where we left off last night if that's ok?" Carmen asked.

"I think we saw everything we needed to see yesterday anyway." Tim added.

We started our walk back to the house, and for a moment my mind drifted back to Shirley, and wished she could have been a part of our discussions. I know she would have loved these two, and she loved to share the Word of God with anyone and everyone. I wondered if seeing Tim and Carmen walking hand in hand would remind her of our youth, as it did me.

As we walked up onto the porch I decided that we were definitely going to need a glass of sweet tea in order to continue this conversation.

"Tim, if you'll help me in the kitchen for a moment I'll fix us some drinks."

"I'm right behind you." He replied.

We prepared the drinks, and returned to the porch where Carmen was kicked back comfortably on her end of the swing waiting patiently. Tim sat down with her, and I took my place in my rocker, with my Bible in hand.

"Ok, you'll have to remind me where we left off, because my memory just isn't what it used to be." I said laughing, but in my mind, knowing it was true.

"You were about to give us the creationists point of view, as opposed to the evolutionists theories." Carmen replied, and I couldn't help but notice she looked as happy as a kid in a candy store.

"Oh yes – the creationist point of view – also known as intelligent design, but don't get hung up on the intelligent design part because there are some strange versions of that as well. Before I start, there are a few more theories that I need to make mention of. I guess we all can agree that the universe is real can't we?" I asked.

"I think that's pretty obvious." Tim replied with a little sarcasm.

"I know that sounded like a stupid question, but there are some who are of the opinion that the universe is merely an illusion, which I think is ridiculous, but never the less real. The Big Bang theory is another possibility – there's the belief that the universe sprang from nothing due to some type of quantum fluctuation, and last but not least, Genesis chapter one says that God spoke everything into existence, which would make him the uncaused first cause I spoke about earlier. I think it's appropriate to use the process of elimination to get our answer, so we'll start by eliminating the illusion theory, because each of us knows that the universe is real, and even the majority of scientists don't buy into this one. That reminds me of a famous quote, which stated 'I think therefore I am.' I can't remember who said that, but just knowing we are able to contemplate the question of our origins, shows that we are here."

I couldn't help but laugh, because of how absurd that theory sounds. I noticed both Carmen and Tim were smiling and shaking their heads also.

"The next one to eliminate will be the universe sprang from nothing theory. Using terms like quantum fluctuation is a way to intellectually step outside most people's understanding and give a theory which people are afraid to ask an explanation of – nothing comes from nothing, so nothing can create anything. I would also like to add that using quantum mechanics to insinuate parallel universes does nothing but push the question of origins into another dimension, which does not answer the question any more than assuming that life began in outer space. As I said before - for something to begin to exist, it has to have a cause equal to or greater than itself, so do either of you think nothing has the ability to create something?" I asked.

Tim replied, "That's definitely a tongue twister, but I have to say that it is also not a logical explanation."

"I've never heard of those two theories, and I can see why – it is anything but logical, however, doesn't the Big Bang theory insinuate that the universe sprang from nothing?" Carmen exclaimed.

"Not exactly." I answered. "In the Big Bang theory, all the matter we know to exist was already in existence, even though they don't understand where it came from, but it was condensed into one place. The big insinuation here is that life and an ordered universe were born from the chaos of an unexplained explosion involving matter that had no explainable beginning and no intelligence to order itself. Let me run in the house and grab something that will help clarify my next point, and I'll be right back." I said, getting up from my rocker. I walked into my office, and after digging through my desk drawer, I found what I was looking for, and made my way back out to the front porch.

I have done a lot of research over the years, and printed out most of the things I have found, and you know what they say, "A picture is worth a thousand words."

"Here's something that will shed some light on our universe." I said, as I handed them the folder, which contained some pictures taken by the Hubble telescope, along with some projection drawings. "These pictures show how the universe appears to be expanding, and believe it or not, support both the big bang theory, and God."

"Do you mean the *Big Bang* and *God* are one in the same?" Carmen asked, with a surprised look.

"What I'm saying is this; The Big Bang theory states that the universe started as an infinitely dense point called a singularity, which contained all the matter and energy known to be in existence. This singularity exploded for some unknown reason, and has been expanding ever since; now the Bible says God spoke the universe into existence and there are many places that describe God stretching out the heavens, which is very much like expansion, so both views would have a starting point, and both fit the expansion model, but only one would have an intelligence driving its expansion and complex organization into the universe we see around us – I lean towards the latter, and who knows, there could have been a *Big Bang* when God spoke his famous words, 'let there be.'" I said loudly while using hand gestures to drive the point home.

"I heard my father once say that if there *was* a big bang, *God* fired the canon." I said as we all laughed at how relevant that analogy really was. "If you'll notice in these pictures how things have a red glow to them; it is due to the light waves being lengthened. With an expanding universe light waves are traveling through space that is being stretched out, which causes the light waves to *decrease* in frequency, or lengthen, and changes the appearance towards the red end of the light spectrum. It also has the opposite effect if something is being compressed, which *increases* the frequency, or shortens the light wave, and the appearance changes towards the blue end of the light spectrum; this is known as Hubble's Law."

Carmen looked very puzzled as she said, "I'll have to take your word for it, because I have no idea what light waves and frequency mean."

"You're not the only one." Tim added.

"I guess I got a little deep there." I said apologetically. "Let me give you something to compare to; have either of you heard of the Doppler Effect?" I asked.

"I remember learning something about that in school, but I've forgotten what it is." Carmen answered.

"Well, you can get a similar effect with sound waves and light waves if an object is moving." I explained. "To give you an idea of what the light waves are doing, let's take the sound of a car's horn blowing – if the car is not moving, and you are stationary, the sound doesn't change, but if the car starts moving away from you the sound changes, because the sound waves are being stretched out; if the car is moving towards you, the sound changes in the opposite direction, because the sound waves are being compressed. The same thing happens with light waves, but instead of hearing the effects – we see them. Does that clear things up some?" I asked.

"Yes it does." Carmen answered, "Now I think I'm on track again; that really helped."

"I would like to add a couple more things about this subject before we move on." I stated. "There are a couple more problems with the Big Bang Theory if God is excluded from the equation, and one is time. It is debatable whether or not there would be sufficient time for events to have taken place, cause the Big Bang, and us be able to see what we're seeing in these pictures – also there is the problem with the type of star they say would be needed to cause the results we know to be in existence today, known as a second or third generation star, which would have a different composition than any star known to be in our universe today. At the end of this unusual star's life it would become what's known as a gamma ray burster, which some claim would trigger events leading up to life as we know it today according to their theory. As far as I know there is no evidence of the existence of such stars, much less the ability to produce life out of non-living matter, but this is another one of those topics that is the center of much debate, even if one of those stars is found. The next problem is temperature; if an explosion took place, then the starting point would be of a higher temperature than the outer areas due to the cooling that takes place as debris is spread farther and farther away from its origin, but this is not what we see in real life. Scientific measurements have shown that the temperature of our universe is almost identical no matter what direction or how far you look, which makes sense if everything was created in one instant by a supreme being. Of course, evolutionary scientists had to make an adjustment to their theory in order to compensate for this, so they added the theory of inflation. They decided that for another unknown reason, the universe must have hyper-expanded at the time of the initial blast – jumping from a very small singularity to this enormous expanse we call our universe, and then slowed down for another unknown reason. This is something else you may want to read up on, because it also gets very deep."

"I'd say so." Tim said, "But it is very interesting."

"I have to say that I really enjoyed studying these things myself, and it never ceases to amaze me just how imaginative people can be when it comes to repairing a flaw in their theories." I replied, "Now back to the creationist viewpoint...if God spoke everything into existence, time nor temperature would be a problem, and we wouldn't need the existence of a very unusual star. It's very possible that when we look into the depths of space and see the red appearance of these galaxies, we're really looking back in time to the creation of the universe. Jeremiah 10:12 says, 'He hath made the earth by his power, he hath established the world by his wisdom, and hath stretched out the heavens by his discretion.' This sounds like a very good example of the stretching of light waves to me, and if this was done very quickly then there is no problem seeing what we see in these pictures at such vast distances. The Big Bang theory, on the other hand, has a problem explaining how we can see this many light years away, along with the uniform heat measurments, given the amount of time they think we've been in existence."

Carmen handed me the folder and said, "So it appears the universe had a starting point, which is logical, and it also appears that something had to start the process of life, so what's next?" Carmen asked.

I thought for a moment, and then asked, "Did you guys know that, the more scientists learn about our universe, the more they realize how perfect the setup is for us to exist?"

"No, what do you mean?" Carmen replied.

"I was reading a book the other day that mentioned the earth's ideal location in our solar system. Among the examples listed was the fact that if we were any closer to the sun we would fry, and if we were farther away we would freeze; also a very interesting point was made about ocean tides – If the moon was bigger, the gravitational pull would cause massive tidal waves destroying large areas of land, and if it were smaller, tidal action would cease, and the ocean would become stagnant thus destroying all life in it. This sounds an awful lot like intelligent design to me. When you have something as complex, and perfectly orchestrated as our universe, it only makes sense that it didn't happen by chance...there had to be a creator and that creator is God who designed this place specifically for our existence. If you think about it, the only reason we're able to think using logic, take part in scientific experiments, and draw conclusions based on these things is due to the fact that there is uniformity in nature. Evolutionary scientists are promoting random natural processes as leading to the creation and complex organization of everything we know, but tell me this, how can we know anything without uniformity? And random is the opposite of uniform."

I picked up my Bible, that I had laid next to my rocker, and turned to Hebrews 11:3 and said, "I'm going to read you a few verses of scripture that reveal God as the creator, and show man's foolish imagination – 'Through faith we understand that the worlds were framed by the word of God, so that things which are seen were not made of things which do appear.'" I then turned the pages back to Romans 1:20-23 and read, 'For the invisible things of him from the creation of the world are clearly seen, being understood by the things that are made, even his eternal power and Godhead; so that they are without excuse: Because that, when they knew God, they glorified him not as God, neither were thankful; but became vain in their imaginations, and their foolish heart was darkened. Professing themselves to be wise, they became fools, And changed the glory of the uncorruptible God into an image made like to corruptible man, and to birds, and four-footed beasts, and creeping things.' I then turned the pages to the book of Psalms 19:1, which states, 'The heavens declare the glory of God; and the firmament showeth his handiwork.' I paused for a moment to let that sink in then explained; "The first verse I read explains that through faith we understand the things we *see* were not *created* by the things we see, but by God. The second group of verses shows that God has revealed his power and existence through his creations that we see, and because of this revelation, we have no excuse not to believe in the creator, and then goes on to describe what sounds an awful lot like what's been happening in our world with relation to man's vain philosophies. The last verse tells how the heavens, and the firmament, which is the universe around us, declare the glory of God."

I could tell Carmen's mind was working overtime as she asked, "If God created the universe, then who created God?"

"This is hard to comprehend with our human mind, but the question "who created this?" leads to "who created that?" and it never ends, so ultimately there has to be an *eternal first cause* which I mentioned earlier, and this cause logically would be transcendent and beyond our full understanding. Evolution goes back to pre-existent non-living matter, and the Bible points to God. It takes a measure of faith to believe in either of these choices, but it doesn't have to be blind faith. Even though scientists have never figured out how life could be generated from non-living materials, they refuse to accept a supreme being as the beginning.

"I thought scientists *had* figured out how to bring about life from chemical processes." Carmen said in a questioning manner.

"What you are referring to is the Miller experiment, which they would love for us to believe created life, however nothing could be further from the truth. If you research how that experiment was orchestrated, you'll see that imaginary atmospheric conditions without the presence of oxygen were in place, as well as an unrealistic trap to protect the amino acids that were to be produced. These amino acids, which are very important in the makeup of proteins, could not be produced in the presence of oxygen, but in an atmosphere without oxygen there would be no ozone layer to protect amino acids from the sun's radiation which creates a very big dilemma. Even though this experiment was unrealistic, it still didn't produce life; you see amino acids are classified as either left handed or right handed, and living organisms are comprised of all left handed amino acids with very few exceptions; when an organism dies, the amino acids revert to an equal amount of left handed and right handed which is exactly what the Miller experiment produced. In essence the experiment symbolized *death* not *life*. I believe most evolutionists have a hard time accepting a supreme being because of their inability to see and touch that being. It seems easier for many to put their faith only in something they can touch, even if they know its man made. John 4:24 says, 'God is a Spirit: and they that worship him must worship him in spirit and truth.' We have to understand that God is a Spirit, and lives outside the boundaries of time and space, so our feeble minds can't comprehend his much higher thoughts and being; we can't think of him as if he were human, because that imposes many limitations on his power, and thus puts him on a level playing field with us, which simply is not the case. Isaiah

43:10 says, 'Ye are my witnesses, saith the Lord, and my servant whom I have chosen: that ye may know that I am he: before me there was no God formed, neither shall there be after me.' Revelation 21:6 states, 'And he said to me, It is done. I am Alpha and Omega, the beginning and the end. I will give unto him that is athirst of the fountain of the water of life freely.' This is God saying that he is infinite – the beginning, and the end. Jesus Christ also said in Revelation 1:8, 'I am Alpha and Omega, the beginning and the ending, which is, and which was, and which is to come, the Almighty.'"

Tim held his hand out in a gesture to stop me and said, "Wait a minute, I'm a little confused. You said God stated he was Alpha and Omega, and then you said Jesus made the same claim, so how can that be?"

Carmen also wanted to add to that question, "That would mean two Gods wouldn't it?"

I smiled and said, "No not quite. There is only one God revealed in three persons within the Godhead – this is called the Holy trinity."

Both Tim and Carmen looked a little lost, and then Tim said, "Ok you've lost me again – What is the Godhead, and what is the trinity?"

We were now getting closer to the ultimate proof that God is real, but I needed to answer these two questions first.

"The Godhead relates to Gods divine nature as a spirit, and this divine nature is revealed in three eternally distinct persons – God the Father – God the Son – and God the Holy Spirit. When Jesus Christ was born, that was God revealing himself in human form, this is sometimes referred to as the *incarnation* of God, and then after the resurrection, the Holy Spirit was sent as a comforter, and teacher for those who are saved. They are all one God, but three distinct personalities. There have been many analogies brought forth to try and explain how you can have one God and three persons, but they all fall short in some way, however, I'll give you one example that may help, but remember, God is way beyond our understanding so my analogy will fall short as well. If you think about space, it has height, width, and depth; three dimensions un-separable and unable to be comingled together. Even though there are three distinct dimensions, there is only one space. The same applies to the Godhead, the Father, Son, and Spirit are one essence, but have three distinct roles in their relationship. Here's a few verses of scripture that reference their deity and distinct person: In Isaiah 43:10 the Father says, 'Ye are my witnesses, saith the Lord, and my servant whom I have chosen: that ye may know and believe me, and understand that I am he: before me there was no God formed, neither shall there be after me.' Then in Hebrews 1:8 the Father says to the Son, 'But unto the Son he saith, thy throne O God, is forever and ever: a scepter of righteousness is the scepter of thy kingdom.' And then Acts 5:3-4 says, 'But Peter said, Ananias, why hath Satan filled thine heart to lie to the Holy Ghost, and to keep back part of the price of the land? While it remained, was it not thine own? And after it was sold, was it not in thine own power? Why hast thou conceived this thing in thine heart? Thou hast not lied unto men, but unto God.'"

"Ok, that's a little hard to grasp." Tim said, "But wouldn't that mean that Jesus was a creation of God just like us? Why did Jesus have to be born anyway? Why didn't God come himself?"

Carmen looked at Tim with surprise and said, "I was just about to ask the same thing – I guess brilliant minds think alike."

"I'll agree with that." I said, "You kids are definitely asking legitimate questions that are making me work, but neither Jesus, nor the Holy Spirit were just creations of God; the only part that was created was the human nature of Jesus which was created at his conception, which we'll get into shortly, but his deity has always been and always will be. The three members of the trinity have all been around from the beginning of time, and that is first referenced in the beginning of Genesis where the Spirit of God moved upon the face of the waters, and then there's plurality in Genesis 1:26 which says, 'And God said, Let *us* make man in *our* image, after *our* likeness: and let them have dominion over the fish of the sea, and over the fowl of the air, and over the cattle, and over all the earth, and over every creeping thing that creepeth upon the earth.' God's use of the words *us*, and, *our* shows that the Godhead has been plural from the beginning." and the reason God the Father didn't come himself in spirit form, can be found in the book of Exodus 33:20-23, where God says this to Moses, 'And he said, Thou canst not see my face: for there shall no man see me, and live. And the Lord said, Behold there is a place by me, and thou shalt stand upon a rock: And it shall come to pass, while my glory passeth by, that I will put thee in a clift of the rock, and will cover thee with my hand, and thou shalt see my back parts: but my face shall not be seen.'"

"So Moses actually saw God?" Carmen asked.

"Well He saw his back parts." I stated. "I believe that the glory of God in spirit form is so great, that this human body could not stand it if it was face to face, but Moses found favor with God and he was allowed this one embellishment. This is one of the reasons why God revealed himself in human form – In the form of Jesus Christ so we could see God in the flesh, but there was a much more important reason for Jesus being born on this earth than just for our pleasure; he came here as the ultimate sacrifice for our sins, and to give us a way to spend eternity with God."

"What about the Holy Spirit?" Tim asked, "You said the Holy Spirit was sent as a comforter, so what does that mean?"

"When a person is saved, the Holy Spirit is sent from God, and dwells within that person, as a witness, a guide, a teacher, and as a comforter in times of peril; the Holy Spirit also works within us helping us turn from our sins, and helps with our understanding of God's will. In John 14:16-17 Jesus says, 'And I will pray the Father, and he shall give you another Comforter, that he may abide with you for ever; Even the Spirit of truth; whom the world cannot receive, because it seeth him not, neither knoweth him: but ye know him; for he dwelleth with you, and shall be in you.' And then John 14:26 says, 'But the Comforter, which is the Holy Ghost, whom the Father will send in my name, he shall teach you all things, and bring all things to your remembrance, whatsoever I have said unto you.' The Holy Spirit is only inside those who are truly saved, and this is one major revelation to the fact that God is real. Since those who are not saved can't have the Holy Spirit, it is hard to convince them that the Holy Spirit exists."

Carmen looked at me as if she wanted to crawl inside my head and flip through the pages of my mind. It was obvious that she was very intelligent, and deep inside I knew that she was seeking God, even if she didn't realize that's what she was doing.

"I have to say, that what you've described makes sense, and it doesn't seem logical that we exist just by chance, so if God *is* who the Bible says he is, did he leave any proof other than creation itself?" She asked.

"Well Carmen, the Bible says creation leaves us with no excuse, but there is more evidence, and it can be found in Jesus Christ."

"But how do we know Jesus even existed? If he did exist, how do we know that he was anything more that a man?" She asked.

I had waited for this moment since our conversation began.

"I'm glad you asked that, because there is a lot of deceit in this world, and I want to share with you the reality of Jesus Christ."

Chapter 4
The reality

"As you probably know, the Christian faith is based on Jesus Christ being the Son of God – who was fully God and fully man – lived a sinless life here on earth – suffered and was crucified on the cross as the ultimate sacrifice for our sins – died and was buried, then rose from the dead on the third day."

They both nodded their heads, alluding to the fact that this is what they had heard in their past, but Carmen's expression revealed a question waiting to be asked.

"Is there something you need to ask, Carmen?" I asked.

"Well, I was just thinking about what you said a moment ago; you said that Jesus is God, but now you said Son of God. I'm a little confused by that." She responded.

"The Bible in many places refers to Jesus as the Son of God, but this is not to be taken in the literal sense as in the offspring of God. This is what's called anthropomorphic language, which helps us to understand the difficult subject of two distinct natures in one person. The human nature of Jesus Christ can be looked at as a son of God, and a son of man, which Jesus referred to himself as many times, because it was created by God at the time of his immaculate conception, but his divine nature is not a creation – it always has been and will be God."

"Ok, I think I understand now. I automatically thought it meant the same thing it means in human terms." Carmen said as she nodded her head.

"Another point that needs to be made is the fact that Jesus came into this world in a supernatural way, which also shows the power of God. Luke chapter 1 describes how God sent the angel Gabriel to visit a virgin named Mary who was engaged to be married to a man named Joseph; God chose her, because she was blessed among women, and highly favored by him. The angel told her how the Holy Ghost would come upon her, and the power of God would overshadow her causing her to conceive."

"Couldn't that have just been a cover up of an affair?" Tim asked.

"Many have thought that same thing." I said, "But the Bible takes care of that in the details. Mathew chapter 1 tells how Joseph was wondering the same thing; he was contemplating putting her away, which means divorcing her, since marriage vows had already been taken upon betrothal in those days, but God sent his angel to visit Joseph in a dream, and it was explained to him about conception by the Holy Ghost, and since Joseph was a Godly man he did as the Lord wanted, and took Mary to be his wife. This is how Jesus could claim to be fully God, and fully man."

"I see what you're saying." Tim added with a nod. "His human part came from Mary, but since he didn't have a human father....the rest of him was God."

"That sounds like a good interpretation to me." I said smiling. "That pretty much tells the Biblical story of his existence, so now I guess I need to prove that Jesus Christ did walk the earth, and then we can move on. Not many people realize this, but even if the New Testament did not exist, we could find most of the same information in liberal, secular, and religious history books, which is something that other religions don't have. It is one thing for Christians to profess all of this, but quite another for non-believers to agree that these people, and places did exist. Have either of you ever heard of Josephus, or Tacitus, or Thallus the Samaritan, or Mara Bar Serapion?"

"None ring a bell." Carmen said.

"I can't even pronounce those names, much less know them." Tim added.

"Each one of these people were historians that wrote about Jesus Christ's existence and crucifixion. Tacitus was a great and very well-known Roman historian who wrote, 'Christus suffered the extreme penalty during the reign of Tiberius at the hands of one of our procurators, Pontius Pilate, and a most mischievous superstition broke out.' – Josephus was a Jewish historian that recorded the early Christian's belief that Jesus had risen from the grave, in his writing of 'Antiquities', and to my knowledge, not a single skeptic, with historical knowledge, has come forth and refuted the existence of Jesus Christ, because there is just too much evidence; even other religions acknowledge Jesus Christ, although they mostly denounce his deity. I'm sure you're both aware that when someone is referencing a year in time, it is followed by either B.C. or A.D."

They both acknowledged their agreement.

"Both of these are references of Jesus' existence, even though many people don't realize it; B.C. stands for before Christ, and A.D. stands for the Latin phrase 'anno domini' which means 'in the year of our Lord', so this in itself shows the impact of his life here on earth."

"You know," Carmen interjected, "all these years I've thought the Bible was the only proof people used for his existence, and I guess when someone says he probably didn't exist, it's because that's an easy thing to say, and most people can't offer any proof otherwise."

"That's a very common response from people, and I only gave you a couple of examples of the historical writings in our archives, but all this information is available in libraries, and online; however, you probably won't see it on the evening news."

"I think I've heard of that Pontius Pilate you mentioned," Tim added, "What was he famous for?"

"Pilate was the procurator at the time of the crucifixion – the Jewish people brought Jesus to him to be sentenced to death, because their laws wouldn't allow them to do it; Pilate found no fault with Jesus, but because of the Jewish custom at that time, he would release a prisoner to the people before the Passover, and the people chose Barabbas the murderer over Jesus, since the Pharisees had all the citizens in such an uproar concerning Jesus."

"It sounds like the Jewish people hated him." Carmen said with a sorrowful look on her face.

"The religious leaders of that time, known as the Pharisees, Sadducees, and chief Priests, did everything they could to turn the people against Jesus, and for many different reasons I'm sure. I believe they thought their careers would be over if Jesus was accepted as the Messiah that had been prophesied about by their own people, but you have to realize that this had to happen in order for salvation to be possible, and God knew these people would carry this out well before Jesus came in human form, so all in all, God's will was done."

"So he did exist, but how do we *know* he wasn't just a normal man?" Tim reiterated what Carmen had asked earlier.

"I'll start by reading a few verses of scripture about Jesus, then I'll give you something to think about – John 1:1 says, 'In the beginning was the Word, and the Word was with God, and the Word was God.' And John 1:14 says, 'And the Word was made flesh, and dwelt among us, and we beheld his glory, the glory as of the only begotten of the Father, full of grace and truth.'"

"I take it Jesus is also known as the Word." Tim stated.

"Yes he is," I responded, "There are many different names that are used to reference Jesus throughout the Bible, and all have their purpose when you truly get into studying it. The last couple of scriptures I'll reference are Colossians 2: 9 which says, 'For in him dwelleth all the fullness of the Godhead bodily.' And then last but not least is John 10:37-38 which says, 'If I do not the works of my Father, believe me not, but if I do, though ye believe not me, believe the works: that ye may know, and believe, that the Father is in me, and I in him.' Now, from the scriptures I've quoted I think it's pretty evident that the Bible claims Jesus to be God, but this last verse is what I'm going to use to take us a little deeper."

"We're already deeper than I ever thought it could get." Tim stated in amazement. "Oh, and by the way," Tim added. "How are you able to recall the locations of all these Bible verses so easily? Do you have the entire Bible memorized?"

"I wish I did, but I have to say no." I laughed, "I've done a lot of reading, and 2 Timothy 2:15 says, 'Study to show thyself approved unto God, a workman that needeth not be ashamed, rightly dividing the word of truth.' Now to someone not saved, studying sounds like a chore, but those who have realized they were lost, repented from their sins, and accepted the wonderful gift of eternal salvation – they can't get enough of God's word. God has shown me how alive the Bible is, and I meditate on it every day."

"I didn't know Christians meditated. I thought sitting in the floor with your legs crossed, eyes closed, and humming was something monks did." Tim said, laughing.

Carmen and I both laughed with him.

"Honey I don't think that is the meditation Jack is talking about – am I right Jack?" Carmen asked.

"I have to say Carmen is right Tim. Meditation is keeping God's word on your mind constantly – Psalm 1:1-2 says, 'Blessed is the man that walketh not in the counsel of the ungodly, nor standeth in the way of sinners, nor sitteth in the seat of the scornful. But his delight is in the law of the Lord; and in his law doth he meditate day and night.'"

"I think I would have a hard time meditating on the Bible, because the wording is very confusing, and sometimes makes no sense to me." Tim stated.

"Well, Tim, you have to keep in mind that the Bible has been translated from the original Greek and Hebrew manuscripts, and we don't talk the same way they did; however, with the help of a good study Bible, a concordance, and most of all, the witness of the Holy Spirit, it will make perfect sense."

"Sorry I distracted you again," Tim said, "I guess you can move on to the next topic now, before I get you even more side tracked."

"No problem," I said, "Philippians 4:13 says, 'I can do all things through Christ which strengtheneth me.' So I should be able to keep things straight, even when other topics come up, as long as I have the Lord on my side. I do hope things are becoming clearer to you, instead of the alternative." I said questioningly.

"Actually I'm very impressed." Tim said, and Carmen nodded her head in agreement.

"Good." I said, "Now I'll give you something to think about; the verse I referenced earlier when Jesus said, 'believe the works' in order to know he is God; Do you have any idea how many miracles Jesus performed while he was here on earth?"

"I have no idea." Carmen answered.

"Don't ask me," Tim added. "I think my lack of studying is evident."

"Well, my study Bible here references thirty seven, even though different references give you different numbers, and there are countless others that the Bible speaks about. These miracles were seen by thousands of people, and that's only the ones we know about; John 21:25 states, 'And there are also many other things which Jesus did, the which, if they should be written every one, I suppose that even the world itself could not contain the books that should be written. Amen.' This tells me that there was a lot more done, and the Bible contains only a tiny portion. There were people healed of lifelong sicknesses, devils were cast out, he silenced a storm, walked on water, fed five thousand people with five barley loaves, and two small fish, raised people from the dead, and many other things. People were coming from near and far, because the word spread quickly of the great things Jesus was able to do – he even healed the ear of one of the Chief Priest's servants, who had come to arrest him, just before his crucifixion."

"Do we really know that these were miracles, and not some sort of scam?" Tim asked.

"As I said earlier, there were thousands of witnesses, and many were still alive at the time the gospels were written, so any discrepancies would have been made public. Now I'm sure that in itself may not satisfy your need for proof of the miracles, so I want to take this a little deeper if you'll indulge me."

"Feel free." Carmen replied.

"Ok, before I continue on with the miracles I want you to look at something else."

I opened my study Bible to the pages that referenced the miracles and prophesies, and handed it to them.

"Have you kids heard of the Prophets of the Old Testament?"

"Yes." Carmen answered, and Tim nodded.

"Well, if you'll notice the pages I've opened up to, there is a list of the miracles performed by Jesus, and also you'll see a list of forty five prophesies – made by Old Testament Prophets – and *all* were fulfilled by Jesus Christ. I read once that the probability of any one man being able to fulfill *most*, much less, *all* of these prophesies, would be astronomical, so think about that while I continue on."

"I can see how this study Bible would be a very useful tool, since it lays everything out for you, and shows references for each topic." Carmen stated, as she glanced at the pages before her.

"I'll have to agree." Tim added. "Maybe this is what I would need to help with the confusion."

I studied the expressions on their faces, and noticed their enthusiasm growing.

"If it will help you kids, I'll make sure you get one." I said smiling, and thankful for the chance to help them. "Alright where was I? Oh yes – the miracles. In order to show that this wasn't a scam, I'm going to use magicians as an example. They make their living by deceiving people with illusions and tricks, but in order to pull these things off, the people who work with them, and are close to them, have to be in on the secrets. Jesus had twelve disciples he had chosen, and they were with him as he performed these miracles; he even gave them power also as it says in Luke 9:1, 'Then he called his twelve disciples together, and gave them power and authority over all devils, and to cure diseases.' Now, if this were a scam they would have to be in on it wouldn't you think?"

"I guess logically they would have to be." Carmen answered.

"Ok, now we're getting to what we Christians call irrefutable proof, which is the resurrection of Jesus Christ from the dead, and *also* something the disciples would have had knowledge of – if it were a scam.

I'm sure you've heard the story, but I'm going to go through it anyway, and hit the high points. The disciples had a hard time understanding all the things Jesus did, and the purposes behind them, so they were not without their doubts about him being the Messiah. After Jesus died, he was taken down, wrapped in burial linens, placed in a tomb, and it was sealed with a stone. The Chief Priests and Pharisees, whom I mentioned earlier, remembered what Jesus said about raising from the dead on the third day, so they asked Pilate for soldiers to guard the tomb, and he consented. On the third day Mary Magdalene, and Mary the mother of Jesus went to visit the tomb, and Mathew 28:2-7 describes what happened, 'And, behold, there was a great earthquake: for the angel of the Lord descended from heaven, and came and rolled back the stone from the door, and sat upon it. His countenance was like lightning, and his raiment white as snow: And for fear of him the keepers did shake, and became as dead men. And the angel answered and said unto the women, Fear not ye: for I know that ye seek Jesus, which was crucified. He is not here: for he is risen, as he said, Come, see the place where the Lord lay. And go quickly, and tell his disciples that he is risen from the dead; and behold, he goeth before you into Galiliee; there shall ye see him: lo, I have told you.' Now the guards, or keepers, later ran to the Pharisees, and described what had happened, which bothered the Pharisees tremendously. They knew that this would have to be silenced quickly, so they paid off the guards to say that Jesus' disciples stole his body while they slept; now, think about that for a second, and tell me if you see a problem with the guard's stories."

Tim and Carmen were both silent for a moment, and then Tim's face lit up with revelation. "How would the guards know the identity of the thieves if they were asleep during all this?" He asked.

"Exactly, Tim." I replied, "This story has never held water for that very reason, and believe me, if the Pharisees thought for one moment that Jesus' body had been stolen, they would have gone to any extreme in order to find it, and make a public display of it to redeem themselves. There was no major campaign launched to find the missing body of Jesus Christ because this lie told by the guards was of their own concoction. No one has been able to undermine his resurrection, and as more proof there were many who saw Jesus before he ascended to Heaven."

"Who saw him?" Tim asked.

"He actually made several appearances to his disciples, and to both Mary's, but the appearance that would serve as more proof to you, is probably the one described in 1 Corinthians 15:6, which says, 'After that, he was seen of above five hundred brethren at once; of whom the greater part remain unto this present, but some are fallen asleep.'

This was a multitude of people, and the majority were still alive when this scripture was written, which adds to its authenticity since the witnesses could be questioned."

Carmen looked a little puzzled as she asked, "How were they able to see him? Wouldn't he have gone on to Heaven?"

"He did not leave his earthly body here as in a normal death. I believe his earthly body was changed immediately to his glorified body, which is something all Christians will receive when he returns the second time. The reason Jesus appeared to all those people was to show his power over death, and also to prove to the people, along with his disciples, that he was who he claimed to be. He then gave his disciples the great commission, and then, Acts 1:4-11 describes his ascension to the right hand of the Father."

"What was the great commission?" Tim asked.

"That can be found in Luke 24:44-47, which says, 'And he said unto them, These are the words which I spake unto you, while

I was yet with you, that all things must be fulfilled, which were written in the law of Moses, and in the prophets, and in the psalms, concerning me. Then opened their understanding, that they might understand the scriptures, And said unto them, Thus it is written, and thus it behooved Christ to suffer, and to rise from the dead the third day: And that repentance and remission of sins should be preached in his name among all nations, beginning at Jerusalem.' In essence, Jesus ordered them to preach the Word of God in his name, and tell everyone all over the world, that forgiveness of sins was available to anyone who put their faith in Jesus Christ, and turned from their sins."

There was one more point I wanted to make to them, which I knew would help them to believe in his resurrection.

"There were many people, including disciples and apostles that were tortured, and killed because they would not turn from their belief that Jesus was the Son of God. Do you think all these people would have been willing to die for a scam?" I asked, hoping they could apply logic to what they've just heard.

"After everything you've brought to our attention, I would have to say that this really happened." Carmen replied, and I could tell that this new information was helping her eliminate some of the corrupt reasoning she'd heard in the past.

Tim also looked like he was coming around – maybe not completely – but definitely coming around. "If only one person was willing to die, then I might say they were delusional, but for many to die, I would have to conclude that they'd really seen irrefutable proof, and were aware of the consequences of denying Jesus."

I was amazed to hear this coming from Tim, after his original opinions, but I also firmly believe in the power of God's Word. I wasn't quite as surprised with Carmen on the other hand, because I couldn't help but think that she had been searching for the truth, maybe for a long time, and was waiting for someone to point her in the right direction.

"That's right." I added, "These disciples and many others had seen Jesus after his crucifixion with there own eyes, and Thomas actually touched him as John 20:27 describes, 'Then saith he to Thomas, Reach hither thy finger, and behold my hands; and reach hither thy hand, and thrust it into my side: and be not faithless, but believing.' Then in verse 29, 'Jesus saith unto him, Thomas, because thou hast seen me, thou hast believed: blessed are they that have not seen, and yet have believed.' These people had experienced first hand, our Lord and Savior; they had witnessed the many miracles, and they had been given power themselves by Jesus, and because this was reality were willing to give their lives – knowing they would spend eternity with Jesus instead of eternal punishment in hell; the rest of us, who have not seen Jesus physically, are blessed for our belief by faith. I would like to reference one more person who is a good example of the knowledge that Jesus Christ overcame death, and that person is the apostle Paul. He is first referenced as Saul before his name was changed, and he was devoted to persecuting Christians, because he believed Christianity was heresy – being taught this throughout his life. He was relentless at trying to put an end to the followers of Jesus Christ by even going door to door, dragging anyone he deemed guilty off to prison. One day on his way to Damascus to continue his persecutions, his life took a dramatic turn; he came face to face with Jesus himself whom he knew to have been crucified, and was asked why he continued to persecute him. Other men who were with Paul, and could hear Paul speaking to Jesus but could see only the bright light that shown about him, were witnesses to this event. Paul was even left blinded by this experience for three days until Jesus sent a man to heal him. This opened Paul's eyes to the reality that Jesus *is* the true Son of God, and Jesus then commissioned him to begin preaching throughout the lands. He went on to do great things for the Lord, even though many who used to be his accomplices were then out to kill him, and he suffered many hardships because of his new belief, but there were countless numbers that turned their lives over to Jesus, because they knew this had to be real in order for someone like Paul who was so determined to kill Christianity, to then make a 180 degree turn in his life. Paul is the perfect example of how Jesus can take someone – no matter how bad they are – and turn them into a new creature. All these miracles, and transformations performed by Jesus led to countless conversions, and because it was so well known to so many people, Christianity spread very far, and very fast."

"I am wondering about one thing." Carmen said, "Jesus could have proved his power by coming down off the cross, and saving himself right there in front of everyone, so why did he go through the pain and suffering?"

Chapter 5
The sacrifice

"Jesus definitely could have saved himself, but then he could not have saved us. When they came to arrest him he said in Mathew 26:53-54, 'Thinkest thou that I cannot now pray to my Father, and he shall presently give me more than twelve legions of angels? But how then shall the scriptures be fulfilled, that thus it must be.' And then in John 10:17-18 he says, 'Therefore doth my Father love me, because I lay down my life, that I might take it again. No man taketh it from me, but I lay it down of myself. I have power to lay it down, and I have power to take it again. This commandment have I received of my Father.' You see – back in the Old Testament, under the first covenant, people would sacrifice an unblemished animal for their sins as a burnt offering to God, which was a foreshadowing of the new covenant to come. God knows man's heart, and knows we can't keep the Law of Moses, so we needed a method of forgiveness and reconciliation. Jesus came here to die as the ultimate sacrifice for our sins, so that we can experience everlasting life with God in Heaven."

"Why did there have to be a sacrifice in the first place?" Tim asked.

"I guess the best way to explain this is to say that God is the supreme judge and he is *just*. It is because he is *just*, that keeps him from overlooking sin, and means a price has to be paid for it. Our judges here on earth sometimes let their own personal beliefs or impulses affect their judgments, because they're human; God, because of his just nature, doesn't have this problem. There never has been, and never will be any human being on earth that is without blemish, and capable of paying the sin debt for everyone, so this is why Jesus was born of woman into this world. He led the sinless life we are incapable of living, and because he had a human nature, he could represent mankind, which qualified him to pay the price for all mankind – all we have to do is accept that payment with faith, and repent."

"I see what you're saying." Carmen said, "It's like when someone gets caught doing something illegal, and then find out someone has already paid their fine – all they have to do is accept the gift, and take their release papers."

"That sounds like a good enough explanation to me." I said, laughing at her enthusiasm.

I noticed a perplexed look on Tim's face, and I wondered what he was thinking. I could tell he was trying to work things out in his mind, and I figured there was another question coming. It wasn't long before he spoke.

"You have done a great job of explaining things to us in a way that makes a lot of sense, but I'm having a little trouble understanding something. Why would God create a being that is going to die, and then hold us accountable for sinning, when he created us this way?"

"Actually Tim, God did not create us to die; we were created for eternity. The curse of death came about after Adam and Eve rebelled against God in the Garden of Eden, and every sin has its consequences; scripture says that the wages of sin is death. The book of Genesis tells the story of how God placed Adam and Eve in the garden, and had given them everything, but he explicitly told them that they could eat of every tree in the garden except of the tree of the knowledge of good and evil. God told them that if they eat of this tree they would surely die, but Satan tempted Eve by telling her that she would *not* surely die. He told her that their eyes would be opened, and they would become like gods knowing good and evil, so she ate the fruit, and gave also to Adam, who likewise ate. After this, they were cursed, as described in Genesis 3:14-21, kicked out of the Garden, and from then on man's days have been numbered. God told them death was the consequence of eating this fruit, and at this time they became mortal. Because we are all descendants of mortal beings, we are mortal also."

"But God created them to sin, so how can it be their fault?" Tim asked, in a defensive manner.

"God didn't create us with sin being our ultimate purpose; he created us with *free will*, and in order for free will to exist, we have to have a choice, and a cognitive ability to choose – otherwise we would be like robots programmed to carry out certain tasks, and that's not what God wants. Let's say you have a child that is of age, and you warn him or her not to get too close to the oven because it's hot, and you don't want him or her to get hurt. Is it your fault if the child waits until your back is turned – reaches for the oven – then starts screaming in pain? No it's not. The child made his or her own mind up to reject your wisdom, and now he or she is paying the price for it. It is the same with God. He wants us as human beings to have our own minds and make our own decisions, so he can have a real relationship with his creation. He has given us warnings, and rules to follow, and it's up to us to heed them. It wouldn't be worth much if we didn't have the choices we have, because he wants to be loved and respected of our own free will, and we all know that love has no meaning if it is forced."

"I guess that makes sense." Carmen stated, with an approving nod of her head. "It would be easy for the creator of the universe to force his creation into subjection, but why would God want that when there's the possibility of the real thing."

"Exactly." I responded enthusiastically. "We all would rather people love us for who we are, instead of them having a relationship with us due to guilt, force, or mere circumstances; there is no joy in knowing that there is no sincerity."

Tim sat there for a moment in silence, but he didn't look confused as he had earlier.

"I guess I've never entertained the notion that an all powerful God would want a relationship with us; I've always thought about God as being cruel, unforgiving, and punishing us for his amusement – I guess that's another reason I've steered away from religion." He said.

"If you don't mind me asking, what made you think God is cruel?" I asked, hoping he would be able to pinpoint where this way of thinking originated.

"I guess it came from church." He replied, as he journeyed back in his mind to childhood. "I remember being told that we would all burn in hell if we didn't come to that altar and tell the preacher all of our sins, so he could intercede with God and forgive us. He would pray that God would hurt people, or make them sick if they weren't in church every time the doors were open, but I always wondered how God could treat people that way, or send someone to a place where they would burn forever if he really loved us, and that preacher always stared at us kids as if he were directing his threats right at us – it made me very uneasy to say the least."

"I can see why you would think that way." I replied, struggling to find the right words to comfort him from the damage that had been done so long ago. "I don't want to make any judgments about the church you attended, since I've never been there, but I do feel that it's necessary to point out anything brought to my attention, that is not Biblical; hell is a very real place that was prepared for Satan and his Angels, then man got added to the list after the fall of Adam and Eve, so it does need to be preached about, however, confessing sins to a preacher will not prevent anyone from going there, and I can't think of any scripture that teaches us to pray bad things about someone who doesn't behave in a manner in which we approve. Going to church is important, but if you're not there, that's between you and the Lord. In the Old Testament, Priests did intercede for the people, but that all changed with Jesus, and the new covenant; Jesus paid our sin debt and only he has the ability to forgive sins – no preacher can forgive you – no preacher can save you. Ephesians 2:8-9 says, 'For by grace are ye saved through faith; and that not of yourselves: it is the gift of God: Not of works, lest any man should boast;' this plainly says that our salvation is not brought on by any work done by man – it is a gift from God. 1 John 1:7-9 states, 'But if we walk in the light, as he is in the light, we have fellowship one with another, and the blood of Jesus Christ his Son cleanseth us from all sin. If we say that we have no sin, we deceive ourselves, and the truth is not in us. If we confess our sins, he is faithful and just to forgive us our sins, and to cleanse us from all unrighteousness.' That scripture states that the blood of Jesus cleanses us from sin….not the preacher, and the confessing it talks about is to God…not man."

"Maybe I misunderstood what the preacher was trying to say." Tim said in an apologetic way.

"That is possible." I said, "But you may not have…you see, not all preachers are called by God. I mentioned false teachers earlier, and false preachers fall into that same category. If he was telling people that he could grant their forgiveness, and save them from hell, then he was not teaching the Word of God. 1 John 4:1-3 says, 'Beloved, believe not every spirit, but try the spirits whether they are of God: because many false prophets are gone out into the world. Hereby know ye the Spirit of God: Every spirit that confesseth that Jesus Christ is come in the flesh is of God: And every spirit that confesseth not that Jesus Christ is come in the flesh is not of God: and this is that spirit of antichrist, whereof ye have heard that it should come; and even now already is it in the world.' Sometimes uneasy feelings are warnings against spirits that are not of God, so they must not be ignored. Another scripture I'm reminded of is in 2 Corinthians 11:4, 13-15 which says, 'For if he that cometh preacheth another Jesus, whom we have not preached, or if ye receive another spirit, which ye have not received, or another gospel, which ye have not accepted, ye might well bear with him. For such are false apostles, deceitful workers, transforming themselves into the apostles of Christ. And no marvel; for Satan himself is transformed into an angel of light. Therefore it is no great thing if his ministers also be transformed as the ministers of righteousness; whose end shall be according to their works."

Tim nodded his head in agreement, and his facial expression was not lacking in promise. "I think those experiences caused a lot of my bad feelings towards church, and religion in general. When I think of church, I automatically associate it with those feelings, but things are different with you, because you don't talk down to us, and you project God and religion in a positive manner."

It gave me a great feeling of satisfaction to know that I had been able to relate to him in a way that has changed his attitude towards God in a positive way, which is what I had hoped to accomplish, because it glorifies the Lord.

"Thank you Tim." I said in complete satisfaction, "You kids have asked some tough questions, but I do appreciate your willingness to entertain a different view. I hate that you had to endure these feelings all these years, but that goes to show you how sneaky Satan is; he has used false teaching and negative feelings to somewhat convince you that neither he nor God existed, and has kept you away from salvation all these years. The good news is that God is greater than Satan, and all of us, and he has brought us together so that you can hear the truth, and as long as you're alive it is not too late to accept what Jesus has done for you; you then can start that relationship with the Lord, and experience a joy that is unsurpassed, even in the midst of tribulation."

Carmen was looking a little anxious, so I decided to engage her again, since Tim and I had done most of the talking lately.

"Carmen, you look like you're dying to jump in on something."

"Is it that obvious?" She asked

"It's just a hunch." I replied smiling, "We've been hogging the conversation for the past few minutes, so I don't want you to feel left out."

"Oh, I don't feel left out; I was just listening, and waiting patiently, however, I would like to back track a little if you don't mind."

"I don't mind at all; as I said before you can ask any question that comes to mind, and I'll try to answer it as completely as I can."

"Well, I want to go back to the *free will* discussion, and talk about the choices. I understand that in order for free will to exist, there has to be choice; I also understand that God represents *good* and Satan represents *evil,* so where did Satan come from? If God created everything, then he had to create Satan, and if he created Satan....was Satan's purpose to give us the choice of evil?"

"One thing I can definitely tell is that you kids are really paying attention, because I am astonished by the depth of your questions. This is helping me just as much as it helps you, because it is really testing my knowledge."

It really was testing me, but this is why Christians must meditate on God's word, so that we can help lead people to Christ, even in the midst of tough questions or situations.

"Colossians 1:16-17 states, 'For by him were all things created, that are in heaven, and that are in earth, visible and invisible, whether they be thrones, or dominions, or principalities, or powers: all things were created by him, and for him: And he is before all things, and by him all things consist.' So yes God did create Satan, but he was not created to be the evil one sitting on your shoulder and whispering in your ear. Believe it or not Satan was created as a very high ranking Angel called a Cherub, and he covered the throne of God."

"You're kidding." Carmen exclaimed with a look of surprise.

"No, I'm really not kidding," I said smiling at her. "God says in Ezekiel 28:14-16 'Thou art the anointed Cherub that covereth; and I have set the so: thou wast upon the holy mountain of God; thou has walked up and down in the midst of the stones of fire. Thou wast perfect in thy ways from the day that thou wast created, till iniquity was found in thee. By the multitude of thy merchandise they have filled the midst of thee with violence, and thou hast sinned: therefore I will cast thee as profane out of the mountain of God: and I will destroy thee, O covering Cherub, from the midst of the stones of fire.' This tells of Satan's role as a Cherub Angel – how he was perfect from his creation, and how he would be thrown out, because of his sin."

"Does the Bible say what his sin was, and why he was thrown out?" Carmen asked.

"Yes it does," I answered, "Verse 17 of Ezekiel chapter 28 says, 'Thine heart was lifted up because of thy beauty, thou hast corrupted thy wisdom by reason of thy brightness: I will cast thee to the ground, I will lay thee before kings, that they may behold thee.' Then back in Isaiah 14:12-15 it says, 'How art thou fallen from heaven, O Lucifer, son of the morning! How art thou cut down to the ground, which didst weaken the nations! For thou hast said in thine heart, I will ascend into heaven, I will exalt my throne above the stars of God: I will sit also upon the mount of the congregation, in the sides of the north: I will ascend above the heights of the clouds: I will be like the most high. Yet thou shalt be brought down to hell, to the sides of the pit.' You see, most people picture Satan to be some hideous thing with horns, a pointed tail, and carrying a pitchfork, *if* they believe he exists at all; The Bible describes Satan to be beautiful and perfect in his ways, but his beauty, and brightness corrupted him, and he became full of himself – he then decided he would exalt himself above God, which caused his downfall."

Carmen contemplated her next question for a moment. "If Satan decided to do this on his own, does that mean the angels were created with free will like us?"

"Good observation," I commended her. "And yes it does; none of God's creations, including the Angels, have been forced to love him – like I said before...God didn't want robots, so even the Angels have free will of some sort. Satan's influence was so powerful that even one third of the Angels in heaven decided to follow Satan instead of God, according to Revelation 12:3-4, which says, 'And there appeared another wonder in heaven: and behold a great red dragon, having seven heads and ten horns, and seven crowns upon his heads. And his tail drew the third part of the stars of heaven, and did cast them to the earth: and the dragon stood before the woman which was ready to be delivered, for to devour her child as soon as it was born.' So we should never underestimate him."

"That was a little confusing." Tim interjected.

"I'm sorry about that." I said, shrugging my shoulders, "If you haven't read all the scriptures in their context, this could be confusing. Satan is referred to as the great red dragon in this passage, and the Angels are the stars of heaven; by saying his tail drew the third part of the stars and cast them to earth, the author is using symbolism to say that Satan took a third of the Angels to earth with him when God cast him out of heaven. The woman who was ready to give birth was Mary, and the child was Jesus himself."

"Ok, I see what you're saying." Tim said. "I've heard that the Bible was a mixture of poetry, history, and symbolism, so I guess this just shows that I haven't read it."

"That's ok Tim; now is as good of a time as any to start, and one thing that will help you more than anything is to ask the Lord to reveal things to you as you go. Jesus said in Mathew 7:7, 'Ask, and it shall be given you; seek, and ye shall find; knock, and it shall be opened unto you:'"

I looked at Carmen and noticed she was ready to burst again with questions, so I held my hand out as a gesture inviting her to jump in.

"I was just thinking about the Angels that followed Satan; where are they now?" She asked.

"They are here on earth helping Satan with his plans of deceit; you may have heard them referred to as fallen Angels or demons?" I said questioningly.

They both nodded their heads.

"They have been called many different names, and even though many probably feel that demons are something Hollywood has made up, I'm sad to say that they are very real."

Chapter 6
Demons around us

Many people, along with Christians, go day to day unaware of the spiritual battle that is taking place in their lives, and all around them. They fail to give Satan and his follower's credit for the attacks on people's minds, including their own, because of their disbelief in his power, or refusal to accept his very existence. If we don't study God's word, in order to be aware of Satan's ways, then we will surely fall of our own ignorance. Ephesians 6:11-12 puts things in perspective; it says, 'Put on the whole armor of God, that ye may be able to stand against the wiles of the devil. For we wrestle not against flesh and blood, but against principalities, against powers, against the rulers of the darkness of this world, against spiritual wickedness in high places.' So studying God's word will prepare us for what's out there."

"So there are real demons walking around on earth with us." Carmen stated with a genuine concern about her as she said this.

"Job 1:7 says, 'And the Lord said unto Satan, whence comest thou? Then Satan answered the Lord, and said, from going to and fro in the earth, and from walking up and down it.' So yes they are here even though we don't physically see them, however, they are confined, and limited in their powers by God; they can only do what the Lord allows them to do. 1 Peter 5:8 says, 'Be sober, be vigilant; because your adversary the devil, as a roaring lion, walketh about, seeking whom he may devour:'"

"Why does God allow him to do anything?" Tim asked.

"Well, as I said before, unless I see the answer written in God's word, I do not want to assume that I know what God is thinking. There could be any number of reasons why – one being that God uses Satan to test our faith and love for him like he did with Job – he could be using Satan's actions as a teaching tool, or he could even use something that's been done to you as an attention getter for someone close to you. The fact is that God is sovereign and he knows what he is doing, even if we don't."

"What happened with Job?" Tim asked.

"Job was a very rich man, he was upright in the eyes of God, and he shunned evil. When compared to most men, Job was a good one, but he was still a man, and every man has faults that he must acknowledge. The story of Job is 42 chapters long, so I'll just give a brief overview. In Job 1:8-12 it says, 'And the Lord said unto Satan, Hast thou considered my servant Job, that there is none like him in the earth, a perfect and an upright man, one that feareth God, and escheweth evil? Then Satan answered the Lord, and said, Doth Job fear God for nought? Hast not thou made a hedge about him, and about his house, and about all that he hath on every side? Thou hast blessed the work of his hands, and his substance is increased in the land. But put forth thine hand now, and touch all that he hath, and he will curse thee to thy face. And the Lord said unto Satan, Behold, all that he hath is in thy power; only upon himself put not forth thine hand. So Satan went forth from the presence of the Lord.'"

"That sounds like Job is going to be punished by God at the hands of Satan." Tim stated with disbelief. I guess he thought this story was going to make God look bad or something.

"He wasn't being punished by God at all, even though it started out looking that way. God had confidence in Job's loyalty and Satan wanted to try and prove God wrong, by thinking that if all Job's riches were taken away, he would then turn on God and curse him, so God used this situation to prove Satan wrong and teach Job a lesson at the same time. He gave Satan power over everything that Job had, but he was restricted from harming Job's person, so the first thing Satan did was destroy Job's livestock, and then his family; instead of cursing God, Job blessed the name of the Lord, and did not sin. After failure during the first round, Satan asked permission to attack Job's health, in order to prove Job would turn on God, and God granted it. Satan caused Job to be afflicted with painful boils from head to toe, and because of the prolonged misery of this condition, Job's wife questioned his allegiance to God, and told him to curse God and die. Job then told his wife that she spoke as a foolish woman, and he remained loyal to the Lord. Word got out about Job's ailment, since he was well known and respected by many people, so some of his friends came to sit with him. They sat with him for seven days and nights before the first one decided it was time to give his opinion. His friends ruthlessly accused him of sinning against God, causing this plague to come upon himself, and they – one after another – attacked his claim of innocence. At times, the pain was so bad that Job wished he'd never been born, and he made several requests for God to take him now, but he never renounced his innocence, and he never cursed God; he did, however, question God's judgment, and became a little too sure of his own righteousness – he even wondered if God had turned him over to the wicked. This is the point I think God was waiting for; he waited for Job to admit how highly he thought of himself, and then it was time to give Job a taste of reality, and bring this thing to an end. God came to them, and spoke to Job from a whirlwind. God enlightened him on just how powerful he is, and how meek man is. After quite a 'talking to' from God, Job had a new appreciation for God's sovereignty and omnipotence, so he then submitted himself totally to God; his health and family were immediately restored, and as a reward for his allegiance, his material possessions were doubled from what he previously had. Now, since Job's friends had wrongly judged him, God also spoke to them about their wrongdoing, and ordered them to bring sacrifices to Job, and he was to pray for them. Jesus explains in Mathew 7:1-5 how we are not to judge self-righteously; It says, 'Judge not, that ye be not judged. For with what judgment ye judge, ye shall be judged: and with what measure ye mete, it shall be measured to you again. And why beholdest thou the mote that is in thy brother's eye, but considerest not the beam that is in thine own eye? Or how wilt thou say to thy brother, Let me pull out the mote out of thine eye; and, behold, a beam is in thine own eye? Thou hypocrite, first cast out the beam out of thine own eye; and then shalt thou see clearly to cast out the mote out of thy brother's eye.' This is not telling us not to judge at all, but it warns against judging someone else when we have sins in our own life that need to be cast out first."

"I guess in the end there were several lessons to be learned by all involved." Carmen said.

"Yes, and if we study this ourselves, we will gain in knowledge also; the Bible is one very important way that God speaks to us, and teaches us what to do and what not to do. This *one* story teaches us not to judge each other self righteously - never to question God's judgment - remember that God is sovereign – never ever decide that we are righteous in the eyes of God no matter how good we try to be, and last but certainly not least, this was one small insight on how Satan works in our lives."

"Since the Bible is how God speaks to people, does it tell us how to deal with Satan?" Tim asked.

"There are many instructions about dealing with Satan," I answered, "But I guess a good way to sum things up would be to take things in the order of the Bible. Satan is first mentioned in Genesis, when he tempted Eve, which gave a small example of the methods he uses against us; in the book of Job we are given more insight about his power over us when permitted, then in the New Testament we are introduced to just how brazen he is when he tried to tempt Jesus, but every time he tried, Jesus would use the Word of God against him, which is the answer to your question. There is always guidance. For example, if you're feeling tempted to lie about something, just remember God's word which says, 'Thou shalt not bear false witness.' "

"I guess that would also back up your statements on studying the Bible." Tim said smiling.

"How right you are Tim." I responded, also with a big smile. "If we don't know God's word, then we won't know Satan's traps, and more importantly, we won't have anything to fight back with. The Holy Spirit will use the Word of God in our minds to show us the will of God in our lives, and provide a defense against Satan's attacks."

"You said Satan tempted Jesus also, so why do you think God allowed Satan to do that?" Tim asked.

"I think it's because we as humans can relate to the physical being of Jesus, and reading about him enduring something that we have to deal with on a routine basis, such as temptation, gives us a little extra push when it comes to fighting Satan; we then can look at temptation – not as a bad thing – but as a chance to do the right thing."

Carmen was sitting there, obviously consumed by her thoughts again. "You know, I've never gave any serious thought to Satan worship; I've always attributed it to some kind of whacky religious act caused by a chemical imbalance in someone's brain, but from what you're saying…people *can* worship him just like they worship God."

"Yes they can." I answered, wishing to myself that more people would realize just how dangerous this kind of thing is. "The occult is very real, and there are many ways that it manifests itself. A few of these practices are: witchcraft, trying to contact the dead, fortune telling, divination, and even some types of astrology. It is spelled out by God in Deuteronomy 18:10-12, which says, 'There shall not be found among you any one that maketh his son or his daughter to pass through the fire, or that useth divination, or an observer of times, or an enchanter, or a witch, or a charmer, or a consulter with familiar spirits, or a wizard, or a necromancer. For all that do these things are an abomination unto the Lord: and because of these abominations the Lord thy God doth drive them out from before thee.'"

"That is pretty straight to the point," Carmen said, and Tim nodded in agreement. "But if these people are worshiping Satan or demons, they must believe God exists also…don't you think?"

"I'm sure some do; even Satan *believes* in God, but he will still be thrown into the lake of fire." I said. "I'm sure there are also a lot of people that are just following their friends, or partaking in these things for any number of different reasons, and have no idea that their playing with fire….literally. The reason many don't have a clue is, because Satan has blinded their minds. 2 Corinthians 4:3-4 says, 'But if our gospel be hid, it is hid to them that are lost: In whom the god of this world hath blinded the minds of them which believe not, lest the light of the glorious gospel of Christ, who is the image of God, should shine unto them.' Satan is referred to as the god of this world in this passage, and since these people don't have God in their lives, Satan is able keep the truth hidden from them."

"I guess Satan don't really care if they know their worshiping him or not, as long as they're not worshiping God." Tim added.

"Very well put Tim." I commended him. "If someone worships Satan he wins, and if someone refuses to believe neither he nor God exists he wins."

"What about someone who is saved? Can Satan take them away from God, or can demons possess a Christian and prohibit them from going to heaven when they die?" Carmen asked.

"No he can not." I replied with utter satisfaction. "When a person has accepted Jesus Christ, and is truly born again, they are in God's family from then on, and Satan can never take them away; he *can* still influence our lives if we distance ourselves from God, and give him the opportunity, but we still belong to God. You will hear some say that you can lose your salvation, and Satan would love for us to believe that, but I don't; I have not found it written anywhere that a person has to be saved over and over, because of sin or anything else. God's word says that we are sealed until the day of redemption, and we are kept by his power – not anything we do. I have often thought about this and I come back to the same conclusion; think about this…what if a person had led a perfect life here on earth, and was the most Godly person ever to exist, other than Jesus, but one day as they were crossing the street a sinful thought crossed their mind, and before they could ask for forgiveness…BLAM! They were run over by a bus. I don't think it would be *just* for that person to be condemned to hell, because they were unable to live a sinless life after being saved, and this one sinful thought caused them to lose their salvation do you? Being saved doesn't stop us from being human, and as humans we are still weak in the flesh, but what people fail to realize sometimes is that it is our soul that's made perfect at salvation and kept by Jesus Christ. This body will die and decay but when Jesus returns he will raise a new body that's incorruptible and not susceptible to sin that will be reunited with our souls."

"I have to say that wouldn't seem fair." Carmen replied.

"Now touching on the human aspect again, a Christian – because we're still human – will still falter sometimes and sin, but a true Christian will not *live* in sin, because Jesus is in our hearts; the Holy Spirit will convict us of our sins, and we will be compelled to repent and ask God for forgiveness. What makes this hard to grasp sometimes is the fact that you see apostasy all around us; people who once professed Jesus Christ as their savior now tell you just the opposite. We have to always keep in mind that not everyone who professes to be saved is actually saved; someone who is truly saved may become rebellious, but they can never truly denounce Jesus Christ. If you can sincerely denounce him then it tells me that you never knew him in the first place. Someone who isn't saved can wander about all over the place because their lost and never had that relationship to begin with. The Bible says those who are truly saved will endure to the end."

"So Satan can't take you away from God, but what about demonic possessions like you see in the movies?" She asked.

"Just like I said before, if a person is truly born again, then God is in them and neither Satan nor his angels can inhabit the same space; light and darkness cannot be in the same place at the same time. 1 John 4:4 says, 'Ye are of God, little children, and have overcome them: because greater is he that is in you, than he that is in the world.' This states that God dwells inside a Christian, and is greater than anything of the world. Now, for a lost person demonic possession is a real possibility and there are many examples in the Bible relating to this very thing."

Tim looked a little perplexed again, "If he can't take Christians away from God, then why bother messing with them?" He asked.

"Actually it's very simple. A person who has dedicated their life to God is a thorn in Satan's side. If they are living a godly life then they will have a positive influence on those around them – possibly leading friends and family to Christ, and this is something that Satan *does not want*, so if he can influence a Christian to sin, it hurts that persons credibility with the people around them, and puts the notion in their heads that this religion stuff is non-sense, and impossible to live up to; on the other end of the spectrum, if he can persuade Christians that it is enough just living a good life, and doing nothing to promote the gospel, he again has prevented someone from being led to Christ, because they are content doing nothing."

"I hadn't thought about it like that, but I see what you're saying." Tim replied. "What you said a moment ago leads me to another question though."

"Ask away." I said.

"You mentioned that someone had to be truly born again. What exactly does born again mean?" He asked.

"A lot of people have trouble with that one," I replied, "and it's because they're thinking about being born in a physical sense, as we all were at one time. People are *physically* born into this world as one of God's creations…not as one of God's children as you will hear many people claim; you don't become a child of God until you are *spiritually* born again through faith in Jesus Christ, and since people are generally saved not knowing a lot about God and his ways, it is compared with starting all over as an infant, and beginning the learning and growing process. This has nothing to do with the physical world at all; it has everything to do with being *spiritually* reborn on the inside, and it happens at the moment when a person truly believes and puts their faith in Jesus Christ as their savior. It is very important that we understand this, because Jesus said in John 3:3 'Verily, verily, I say unto thee, Except a man be born again, he cannot see the kingdom of God.' In essence, being born again is referring to a spiritual birth, and is very important since God has to be worshiped in spirit and in truth."

"When you say 'by faith' I guess you mean believing that Jesus is real?" Tim asked.

"That's part of it." I replied. "You must believe that Jesus Christ is God in the flesh – revealed to us through the Bible – and believe that Jesus Christ came into this world to pay our sin debt with his life, and then rose from the dead on the third day, proving his deity; you then must accept his gift of salvation by confessing that faith to others and repenting (or turning) from your sins to pursue a relationship with God. Faith is not merely stating a belief in something, but actually believing it in the most comprehensive sense of the word. The Bible's description of faith can be found in Hebrews 11:1 which says, 'Now faith is the substance of things hoped for, the evidence of things not seen.' In this verse *substance* is like *assurance,* and *evidence* is a *realization.* . I can't illustrate enough how *important* faith is, but I'll give you another scripture that will help some more, and that is Hebrews 11:6 which says, 'But without faith it is impossible to please him: for he that cometh to God must believe that he is, and that he is a rewarder of them that diligently seek him.' Does that make sense?"

"It does." Tim answered, "Faith is believing in him as God and savior, as opposed to just believing he exists, even if you can't see him, and we must believe that the Bible was given to us by him as a way of communicating what he desires of us."

"It sounds like you've got it but remember it's not a blind faith; it's not as though you are believing in some fable just for the sake of believing in something…God has already manifested the knowledge of his existence in all of us and will make himself real to you if you let him." I said smiling. "If someone tells you that they are a Christian, but they don't believe that there's an inspired Word of God, or that God is sovereign, or that Jesus Christ is God in the flesh, then something is very wrong; when it comes to God's Word I myself would have a hard time believing in a God that couldn't get the facts right in his one and only instruction manual. Now, the Bibles we have today are translations of the original manuscripts, which are the inspired Word of God, so if you're reading some questionable translation where there's no witness of the Holy Spirit, I suggest that you dig a little deeper and find out if the translation matches the context of the original. This is why I stick to the King James Version; it's as close to the original as you can get – in my opinion."

"I have to admit that up until now, I thought the Bible was full of mistakes myself, and I know many others who believe the same thing." Carmen interjected, "So can you give us more information on this topic; you mentioned earlier that we would touch on this again."

"Sure we can; now is as good of a time as any." I said with a cheerful expression.

Chapter 7
Back to the Bible

"We talked earlier about the Bible being written by man and about how some think it's full of errors - so how can we believe it? Some think that because the Bible was written so long ago, and has been translated so many times since, that it must be full of mistakes, but one of the many things that support the accuracy of our Bible is all the early manuscripts that are still in existence, along with overwhelming archaeological and historical evidence, which support the Biblical people, places, and events. I've even read that there is more evidence supporting the life of Jesus Christ than there is the existence of Julius Caesar, even though you never hear anyone doubt his existence."

"You're kidding." Tim stated with a look of surprise on his face.

"Actually Tim, no I'm not. I think the reason is God planned it that way. God is not going to allow his son and our savior to come here, die for our sins, and not make an enormous imprint on history. If his very existence had faded away long ago, then that would be problematic for a humanity that can only be saved by the messiah, but in actuality Jesus was talked about well before he came, and he will be talked about until he comes again; Acts 3:18-21 says, 'But those things, which God before had showed by the mouth of all his prophets, that Christ should suffer, he hath so fulfilled. Repent ye therefore, and be converted, that your sins may be blotted out, when the times of refreshing shall come from the presence of the Lord; And he shall send Jesus Christ, which before was preached unto you: Whom the heaven must receive until the times of restitution of all things, which God hath spoken by the mouth of all his holy prophets since the world began.' You see, not only does the Bible show how all these prophecies were fulfilled, but history also supports the Old Testament prophesies made hundreds of years before the events took place, which, is another thing that support the Bible and Christianity."

"Speaking of prophecies," Carmen jumped in. "I don't think Nostradamus was a Christian, but didn't he make prophecies that have come true?"

"Nostradamus's works are known as the Quatrains, and I don't think anyone really knows what he was writing about. After reading some myself, I can see how very strange they are. I also watched a documentary on him the other day, and after comparing what I've read, with what I've seen, I'm not sure what to think about Nostradamus. Apparently his writings started out as a sales gimmick to promote an almanac, because he had found that people loved to read this stuff. According to some historians, his writings were very strangely worded, and the old language he used is extremely hard to translate. One of the translators used a sentence out of one of his publications, as an example, and was able to give it three different meanings. Because of the wording, and lack of content, even people who have been studying his writings most of their lives, aren't sure of the intent of his work. This lack of accuracy means that it would be very easy to make one of his Quatrains fit some disaster that has happened in the years since his death, passing it off as a fulfilled prophesy, and since we can't ask him what he was really saying, it will probably always remain a mystery."

"Do you think he was a scam artist or something?" Carmen asked.

"I don't think we can be certain what he was doing, so I'll refrain from making a decision on that, but I do know that people today are misquoting, and rearranging his words to make us think that his prophecies were accurate. I'll give you an example; do you remember some publicity after the attacks on the World Trade Center that stated, 'Nostradamus predicted the 9/11 attacks?"

"I didn't see anything, but I do remember hearing that." Carmen answered.

"I remember hearing about it too." Tim added. "It had a lot of people freaked out."

"Well, the Quatrain they were referring to said this:
In the city of God there will be a great thunder,
Two brothers torn apart by chaos, while the fortress endures,
The great leader will succumb,

The third big war will begin when the big city is burning.

"At first this sounds like the real deal but if you analyze this line by line, it could mean almost anything." I said, knowing there was more to this story, but I wanted to see if they would try to defend this prediction.

"You have to admit, that sounds like it could have been a real prediction, and maybe critics are just tearing it apart, because they don't like him." Tim said with intensity in his voice.

"I have to agree." Carmen added. "It sounds very plausible to me."

"Well, what would you say if I told you that this Quatrain was a hoax?" I asked.

"I don't know, was it?" Carmen asked.

"Yes." I answered. "I just wanted you to see how easy it is for someone to broadcast falsities, and then how eager we can be to defend this falsity without any knowledge or basis of its authenticity. This did look very similar to some of the writings of Nostradamus, but it was actually written by a student, and his purpose was to show how vague Nostradamus's writings were, and how they could have multiple meanings."

"Nice set up." Tim said, shaking his head. "We fell for that one didn't we?"

"I'm sorry about that." I said apologetically. "I figured that would be a good way to prove a point, and have a lasting impression. I also want you to know that there are a lot of other misquotations out there, and the next time you're on the internet, check out some of the sites that are dedicated to exposing falsities."

"So are we to believe that none of his writings hold water?" Tim asked.

"Well, like I said, no one really knows what he was writing about – some say his writings were vague, and written in some kind of code, because he was afraid of being brought before the religious inquisition of that time period, but actually it has been shown that he had a good relationship with the religious leaders, and he wasn't practicing anything that would make him guilty of a crime. It has also been discovered, in recent research, that some of his prophecies were actually paraphrases of Biblical prophecies that are known to have taken place."

"Was he just using Biblical events as a sales tool for his books?" Carmen asked.

"Who knows," I answered. "Because of his methods, many refer to his prophecies as 'retroactive clairvoyance', meaning that his prophecies are great at predicting events that have already happened, or are inevitable. No one has actually been able to use one of his Quatrains to predict an event *before* it happens; they use the Quatrain after an event has taken place, and try to make it fit as a prediction."

"This kind of thing can lead to pandemonium." Carmen added.

"Yes it can." I answered. "There are people using his writings to predict the end of the world, and you know there will be some cult or religious extremist out there who will use this as propaganda in leading their followers into some kind of mass suicide or something."

"People just don't think about the effects of their actions on other people do they? I'm sorry I got you side tracked again, but that was very interesting to hear." Carmen explained. "You can get back to the Bible now, if you want to."

"You can side track me all you want to." I said smiling. "Let's see, where was I? I think I was talking about the support of history for the prophecies, and I also want to say that all 66 books of the Bible are complementary of each other, even though they were written by many different authors over a very long period of time, originating over a thousand years before Jesus was even born, and the main focus is the life and purpose of Jesus Christ – even the Old Testament before his birth for-told the events, and purposes of his coming. There is always going to be disagreements on some of the non-essential elements of scripture, because we as humans tend to make things more complicated than they need to be, but the fundamentals are plain; when you hear someone say that the Bible is full of mistakes or inaccuracies, it most of the time means that attention was not paid to the context of the scripture in question. We have to realize that the Bible is written in several different literary styles, and it is very important to know what style your reading, and how it would have come across to its original audience in order to interpret it correctly. It's just like other pieces of literature in the sense that, it contains poetry, history, metaphoric representations, and symbolism among others, and must be approached with this knowledge in order to get the big picture. Let's take Mathew 4:19 as an example – it says, 'And he saith unto them, Follow me, and I will make you fishers of men.' This is Jesus speaking to Peter and Andrew, who were fishermen by trade, so do you think Jesus was going to show them what lure to put on their fishing rods, in order to catch men?"

"I would say that he was using symbolism that actually meant he would show them how to lead people to God." Carmen answered with a smile that acknowledged her pride in knowing she had deciphered this verse.

"Excellent answer, Carmen." I said, and I was very happy to know that things were starting to come clear to them. "This was a non-controversial verse that I used as an example, but there are many scriptures just like this in the Bible that are somewhat controversial, and people will twist them in many directions, in order to try and discredit its meaning. In most cases where there is a verse in question – *if* there is a verse at all – clarification can be made just by reading the preceding, and or proceeding verses, or chapters in order to find the correct context, but most of the time if you ask someone to point out the inaccuracies, they will not have an example, because they're only repeating what they've heard from someone else."

"That's kind of like our insinuation earlier, about mistakes in the Bible – even though we had no examples to give you." Tim stated.

I was glad to see that they were getting the big picture here, instead of going on the defensive about remarks they had made earlier.

"That's ok Tim; now hopefully you are seeing things in a different light, and if you are in question about anything, I trust that you will dig a little deeper to find the truth, instead of just accepting what you hear, read, or see. I gave you kids several scripture references earlier about the Bible's divine origin, including: 2 Timothy 3:16-17, 2 Peter 1:20-21, and 2 Samuel 23:2, which, speak for themselves, but I'm going to give you a few more verses to contemplate on, and that's 1 Corinthians 2:9-14. This is the apostle Paul speaking, and giving another reference to the origin of Biblical teachings, and then verse 14 describes why people who don't have the spirit of God in them, will not understand what they read; it says, 'But as it is written, eye hath not seen, nor ear heard, neither have entered into the heart of man, the things which God hath prepared for them that love him. But God hath revealed them unto us by his Spirit: for the Spirit searcheth all things, yea, the deep things of God. For what man knoweth the things of a man, save the spirit of man which is in him? Even so the things of God knoweth no man, but the Spirit of God. Now we have received, not the spirit of the world, but the spirit which is of God; that we might know the things that are freely given to us of God. Which things also we speak, not in the words which man's wisdom teacheth, but which the Holy Ghost teacheth; comparing spiritual things with spiritual. But the natural man receiveth not the things of the Spirit of God: for they are foolishness unto him: neither can he know them, because they are spiritually discerned.'"

"So, if I understood that correctly, that means understanding comes by way of the Holy Spirit." Carmen stated.

I could tell she wasn't sure about this one, and by the look on Tim's face, he wasn't either; both of them were looking for confirmation of their interpretation.

"There are many things in the Bible that anyone can understand, but a spiritual acceptance type understanding only comes by way of the Holy Spirit. If someone is genuinely searching for God, he *will* reveal little things here and there to help them, and once a person has experienced salvation, they are given the gift of the Holy Spirit, which dwells within them, and becomes their teacher. The spiritual mysteries that God has for us can only be discerned as a result of the Holy Spirit, and therefore our understanding is because of that discernment and teaching, which begins at salvation, and continues throughout the rest of our lives. There's an old hymn that you may remember from you're childhood church experiences that's titled 'He's still working on me' do you remember that one?" I asked.

"I remember singing that as a kid." Tim answered, and Carmen nodded in agreement.

"Well, this is what the song is talking about; the Lord will continue to teach and nurture his children, for the rest of their lives; sanctification is taking place as long as we are here on this earth. Every day I'm growing and maturing in my relationship with the Lord, and with maturity comes the gift of wisdom, however, because we have free will, we must choose to develop our relationship with God – if we do not pursue it, spiritual maturity will not happen."

"I guess you get out what you put in." Tim remarked.

"I would say that is an accurate observation." I said. "And in this case more is definitely better. In Mark 4:24 Jesus says, 'And he said unto them, Take heed what ye hear: with what measure ye mete, it shall be measured to you: and unto you that hear shall more be given.' I don't know about you, but I want to be in the category of those who *hear* so that more understanding will be given unto me."

"As usual you have done a great job of explaining things, Jack." Carmen commended.

"I agree." Tim added, but it was obvious that he had more to say about this topic. "However, there is one more thing I need to ask about the Bible, before we move on. I don't know if this is true or not, but I heard someone say that there were books intentionally left out of the Bible, because religious leaders didn't want people to see what was contained in them. Do you know anything about that?"

"Yes, I am familiar with that, and you're referring to what some call the lost books of the Bible, and others call the Gnostic Gospels. Many of these books were discovered in a Library of ancient texts called Nag Hammadi in Egypt. "

"I think you're right; that term sounds familiar." He added.

"Have you ever heard the term canon?" I inquired.

They both shook their heads.

"The term *canon* is used to describe a method of determining the authenticity of scripture, or more precisely, the standard. All the books that were determined to be authentic – based on such things as apostolic evidence, time period, and most importantly….inspiration by God, were put into the canon known as the Holy Bible, and thus became the standard. There are 66 books that were included, however, there were some books originating in the first century, and many that came about much later – Christian and non-Christian – that did not make it in, because they were not inspired by God, and did not have any direct

102

roots to the prophets before Jesus or the Apostles who were with Jesus as he walked this earth; contrary to the belief of some, many of these books were complimentary of the Bible, and contained a lot of historical evidences, but the Bible was *only* to contain the Word of God – not the words of man. Proverbs 30:5-6 says, 'Every word of God is pure: he is a shield unto those who put their trust in him. Add thou not unto his words, lest he reprove the and thou be found a liar.' If we put things in the Bible that don't belong, or if we reword things to make them mean something different than God's original intent, then we are in danger of reproof, and we will not be able to defend it to others, which will inevitably discredit scripture as a whole."

"Were there some that disagreed with the Bible?" Carmen asked.

"Of course there were, and books like that are still being written today, but if it wasn't inspired by God, then it wasn't included. The Bible itself actually mentions quite a few books that were not included, such as the book of Jasher that is mentioned in the books of Joshua and 2 Samuel, along with 2 Chronicles 33:19, which mentions the sayings of the *seers*, so it's not like the Bible condemned every other book that was written; some were good, and others were intended to divert people from true Christianity, maybe because they didn't want to be held to anyone else's standard but their own, but no matter how good or bad the book was, it could not be considered God's Word without inspiration by God, and direct decent from God himself – namely Jesus Christ. To sum it up, there were many religious authoritative figures from different denominations, who worked together and overwhelmingly agreed on the 66 books that we call the Bible, because of their use in the churches from the beginning. These church counsels didn't invent the canon at that time but just made what was already known official, and I'm sure we have exactly what God wants us to have, because neither Satan nor his followers can stop God's will from being done."

"I've been so caught up in this that I didn't realize how late it has gotten." Tim stated with surprise. "I need to call the garage and see what's going on. My cell phone should be charged by now, so I'm going to run inside and do that."

"Make yourself at home," I said. "And I hope they have good news for you."

"I guess we need to start thinking about something to eat, because it's already 7:30." Carmen explained. "I would like to try another restaurant downtown. Would you like to go with us Jack?"

"I think I'm just going to have something light, and then hit the bed early." I answered with a slight yawn. "After last night, I could use a little extra sleep."

Tim walked back onto the front porch, a couple of minutes later, to deliver the news, "One of the salesmen said the part came in just before the service department closed for the day, so they should start working on it in the morning. It looks like we'll be with you one more night if that's ok Jack."

"Of course it is." I said. "I've really enjoyed your company, and the conversation."

"You know, I never thought I would say that I enjoyed anything religious, but I have to say, this has really captivated me, and I hope we have time to talk some more." Tim explained.

"Maybe we can continue in the morning," Carmen interrupted. "We're going to go get something to eat, and let Jack get some rest, since we haven't let him breathe since we've been here."

"You're not going with us?" Tim inquired.

"No, you kids go on; I'm going to hit the sack early so we can talk again in the morning, before your jeep gets fixed. I'll leave the front door unlocked, so you just come and go as you please; don't worry about me I sleep like a log." I laughed, but it was so true.

"Ok then, if you change your mind and want us to bring you something back, here's my cell number."

Tim handed me small piece of paper that he'd written the number down on.

"You kids enjoy yourselves, and don't get into any trouble."

"I think we can manage that...see you in the morning."

They walked off the porch – hand in hand again – and both looked happy as ever. I was very content with the way things had gone, and it seemed that maybe when this is over, their lives would forever be changed. I would save them myself if I could, but that is between them and the Lord. I could sleep soundly, knowing that the seed had been planted, and with a little nourishment, who knows what can blossom.

Chapter 8
The last day

I woke up Friday morning feeling so refreshed and invigorated. I do love my sleep, and getting in bed early was the best thing I could have done. After getting a shower I made my way to the kitchen to start a pot of coffee, and this time as I passed the grandfather clock, it read 7:00 a.m. – much better that the late hour I had seen yesterday. The kids were still in bed apparently so when the coffee finished I quietly made myself a cup, and eased out onto the front porch. The town was slowly starting to come alive again, and I noticed the food vendors were busy selling breakfast sandwiches, and hot coffee. The crowds would surely multiply as the day went on, because it was Friday, and the start of the weekend.

As I sipped my coffee, and began the process of waking up, I wondered where our conversation would take us that day. I knew there were still many questions on their minds, and I was sure there would be many left unanswered due to our lack of time; I could only hope that they would continue to pursue the truth as our journey would surely come to an end. I wondered if God would put someone else in their lives to continue where I left off.

My thoughts came to a halt when I heard the screen door behind me screech as it opened slowly.

"Good morning." I said to Carmen as she quietly stepped out onto the porch; she was yawning, and her eyes were barely open.

"Good morning to you too." She smiled back. "Tim is still sleeping, but I couldn't lay there any more."

"Did you keep him out too late last night?" I asked.

"No. We were back by 10:30, but it don't matter what time we go to bed, he can sleep all day if left alone."

"That sounds like me a few years back." I explained. "Now it seems like every day gets a little shorter, so I try to get up a little earlier to make up for it."

We talked for a while about their activities after they left me, and about how it looked like it was shaping up to be another beautiful day, then decided that we would go downtown and pick up some breakfast, and surprise Tim.

We left a note, and began our trip down to one of the food vendors. As we were walking back up the driveway – holding onto the bags of very flagrant food – I noticed that Tim had finally decided to wake up, and was waiting for us on the porch.

He looked very excited, and his eyes were fixated on the bags. "You guys read my mind." He said smiling with utter joy. "I am starved, and I was hoping we were all on the same page."

"Well, we all know how much you like food." I said with a laugh.

"Yes darling, we don't want you to shrivel up and blow away due to lack of substance." Carmen added, grinning from ear to ear.

We thoroughly enjoyed our breakfast out on the porch – people watching at the same time, and as we finished, Carmen looked at me with serious, but cheerful eyes.

"So, what are we going to talk about this morning?" She asked.

"Well, now that I have a full stomach, I think I'm ready for whatever you kids can throw at me." I answered playfully.

I was surprised that Tim had the first question, seeing how eager Carmen was to get started.

"I was wondering about something last night before I went to sleep." He explained. "I know Jesus is an important part of Christianity, but what about someone who doesn't want to associate with organized religion? They *do* believe there is a God, and maybe they've dedicated their lives to doing good things and helping people, but will they go to heaven in the end? The reason I thought about this is, because I know there are people out there who are not Christians, however, they do just as good, or even better than some who do claim to be Christians."

"One thing to keep in mind is that not everyone who *claims* to be a Christian *is* a Christian, but even so, there are some *very* good people out there that do some *very* good deeds, however, works will *not* get you into heaven. We also need to realize that no matter how good we try to be....we are not righteous in God's eyes, unless the blood of Jesus has been applied to our account. I'm going to administer a little test that I once heard on a radio show, and it will show that we are not as good as we think we are, and this will affirm the fact that we all are in need of a savior. Are you willing to participate?" I asked.

"Sure." Tim answered.

"Ok Tim, I'm going to ask *you* the questions, but Carmen I also want you to answer them in your own mind so that it will be clear to both of you."

They both nodded their heads.

"The scenario is that you have died, and you are now standing in front of God to be judged. Would you consider yourself to be a good and upright person – worthy of admittance into heaven?"

He thought for a moment then said, "I know that I'm not the best person in the world, but I definitely am not the worst, so I would have to say that I'm on the good end of the spectrum."

"Ok, let's just test you out on that. How many lies do you think you've told in your life?"

"Way too many to count but everyone has lied at some point, and if they don't admit that they're probably lying." He said defensively.

"That's very true, but everyone is not on trial here….just you. What do you call someone who lies?"

"A liar." He said.

"That's right, now have you ever stolen anything regardless of its monetary value, and I mean anything that wasn't yours? It could even be something as simple as an ink pen bought by your company that you took home with you without permission."

"I probably stole a few little things when I was a kid, but I haven't done that in many years. As far as office supplies go, I guess I never looked at that as stealing."

"Time frame doesn't matter, just the act itself, because God is aware of everything we do or have done, so what do you call someone who steals?"

"A thief."

"Now, have you ever looked at something someone else possessed, and desired it for yourself?"

"Sure all the time, but who doesn't? And what's wrong with that?" He asked defensively.

"To want something someone else has is called coveting, which God warns us against, and since we're on the wanting subject, have you ever looked at a woman and had lustful thoughts about her?"

I noticed this question really got Carmen's attention and she was staring at Tim intently awaiting his response. I decided that I might need to step in and help him out with this one. "I see that you are very interested in how Tim is going to answer this question Carmen, but let me assure you that I already know what his response will be, because men are *very* visually responsive by nature, so it in *no way* diminishes his feelings towards you." I said assuring her

"I'm sorry," She said, dropping her head. "I didn't mean to look as if I were about to pounce on him; I guess I just don't want to think about him looking at another woman."

Tim reached around her to hold her, and said, "Baby you know that I am all yours no matter what impulsive thought may run through my mind, and if I'm to be honest here, I would have to say that my thoughts have gotten pretty distasteful at times."

She smiled as she said, "I know you love me, it's just hard to understand sometimes, since women aren't as visual as men."

"Men and women will probably never totally *understand* each other, but we can *accept* one another's differences, and that will lead to a much happier relationship." I smiled at the two of them. "I'm going to ask one more question, and we'll stop there. Have you ever harbored anger in your heart toward someone?"

"Of course," He said. "I don't think anyone can deal with people on a routine basis without ever getting angry with them."

"That is very true, and as I've always believed, people will eventually let you down. Now I'm going to take these five answers that you gave me, and compare them to God's commandments. Since he's the judge, it's his laws that matter."

"This should be interesting." Carmen said, shaking her head.

"You admitted that you lie, and God says 'thou shalt not bear false witness' – you're guilty of theft, and God says 'thou shalt not steal' – you've admitted to desiring the possessions of others, and God says 'thou shalt not covet' – you've also said that you've harbored anger in your heart, and Jesus says in Mathew

14:19 'For out of the heart proceed evil thoughts, murders, adulteries, fornications, thefts, false witness, blasphemies:' so murder can take place from within the heart, and God said 'thou shalt not kill' and last, but not least, Jesus said in Mathew 5:28 'But I say unto you, that whosoever looketh on a woman to lust after her hath committed adultery with her already in his heart.' And God says 'thou shalt not commit adultery' Now these were only five of the ten commandments, and you've admitted to breaking every one of them, so do you think you would be innocent or guilty in the eyes of God?"

"If I'm judged according to that, I guess I would be guilty, but no one can live up to those standards."

"That's exactly right, and yes *everyone* would be guilty because we will be judged according to God's word – not man's, and just as the Bible says, 'All have sinned and come short of the glory of God' however, we don't *have* to be condemned for our lack of ability to uphold God's commandments, because of what?" I asked, hoping they would know the answer.

"Because of Jesus." Tim replied.

"Exactly. This is why he had to die on the cross. He wasn't forced to do so, but because of his love for the human race he had to take the punishment for our crimes in order for us to be reconciled to God. He *did* uphold the law by leading a sinless life here on earth, and then he took the punishment we deserved for *all* of our sins, so that we would have an intercessor with God the Father. God knows that there are *no works* of any sort that would be worthy of paying our sin debt, so he took care of it for us, because he is a *just* God. Sin has to be paid for and if Jesus hadn't been willing to pay, we would be held accountable."

"I guess it's a good thing he did," Tim said, "because it wouldn't seem fair not to give us a way to pay the debt."

"God will always do right….we just have to get it through our thick heads that we cannot do this on our own – by any of our means. On the judgment day, there are going to be countless people who are unpleasantly surprised that their good works did not save them. In Mathew 7:21-23 Jesus says, 'Not every one that saith unto me, Lord, Lord, shall enter into the kingdom of heaven; but he that doeth the will of my Father which is in heaven. Many will say to me in that day, Lord, Lord, have we not prophesied in thy name? And in thy name have cast out devils? And in thy name done many wonderful works? And then will I profess unto them, I never knew you: depart from me, ye that work iniquity.'"

"That's a pretty harsh thing to hear on judgment day – especially for someone who has tried to live a good life." Carmen said.

"Yes it is, but would you rather hear the harsh truth now, or would you rather someone sugar coat things, and re-word them to sound more pleasing to the ears, only to hear Jesus say go away, because he never knew you?"

"I will definitely take the *truth now* option." She replied.

"Good answer." I said, "It is clarified even more in Ephesians 2:8-9 which says, 'For by grace are ye saved through faith; and that not of yourselves: it is the gift of God: Not of works, lest any man should boast.'"

She pondered what that meant for a moment, and then nodded with a smile, "Boasting sure sounds familiar; people do love to brag on themselves whenever they think they've accomplished something."

"Yes they do, and that's exactly what would happen if works got us into heaven," I added. "There would be people declaring how much more they deserved glory over the next person, because they themselves were *so* much better in their works. The main point here is that salvation is a gift from God, and it's only by his grace, and the willingness of Jesus Christ to give his life as payment for our sins, that we are able to spend eternity with God. If we were able to do this on our own, it would mean that Jesus would have suffered and died in vain."

"That makes sense." She said, nodding her head in agreement. "Salvation by works would have eliminated the need for Jesus to die."

"Now don't get me wrong, there is nothing wrong with good works, in fact we are supposed to do good works; James 2:14-18 says, 'What doth it profit, my brethren, though a man say he hath faith, and have not works? Can faith save him? If a brother or sister be naked, and destitute of daily food, and one of you say unto them, depart in peace, be ye warmed and filled;

notwithstanding ye give them not those things which are needful to the body; what doth it profit? Even so faith, if it hath not works, is dead, being alone. Yea, a man may say, Thou hast faith, and I have works: show me thy faith without thy works, and I will show thee my faith by my works.' You see, when you have the Holy Spirit within you, there is a desire to do good works; it's like a side effect of being saved, and if someone comes to you hungry and in need of clothes, there's no profit in turning them away, but there is fulfillment when you reach out and help them, because this is what the Lord teaches us to do. Another scripture to reference is 1 John 3:17,18 which says, 'But whoso hath this world's good, and seeth his brother have need, and shutteth up his bowels of compassion from him, how dwelleth the love of God in him? My little children, let us not love in word, neither in tongue; but in deed and in truth.' God's love promotes good works in his children, so you might say that faith and works go hand in hand – evidencing one another, and two sides of the same coin; works without faith is dead, and faith without works is also dead. You have to also keep in mind that just having faith in the existence of God will not grant access to heaven, because even Satan and his angels believe in God just as James 2:19-20 says, 'Thou believest that there is one God; thou doest well: the devils also believe, and tremble. But wilt thou know, O vain man, that faith without works is dead?'"

"So believing is not enough?" Carmen said in a questioning manner.

"That's right. As I mentioned before, faith goes much deeper than just believing in the existence of someone or something." I replied, "You must realize your need for a savior, put your whole faith in Jesus Christ as God and Savior, and repent in order to be born again, otherwise, Satan would be spending eternity in heaven too, just for believing that God exists. The works will come natural to someone who follows God. The Bible also alludes to different levels of reward in heaven based on what we do here, which is another reason to live your lives according to the will of God. Jeremiah 17:10 says, 'I the Lord search the heart, I try the reins, even to give every man according to his ways, and according to the fruit of his doings.' There are many more that speak of this, but that's a good one to start with."

"So how can you tell if someone is saved or not, since good works can be done by anyone?" Tim asked.

"That's very simple actually," I answered. "It all boils down to the fact that it is *not* our job to determine if someone *is* or *is not* saved; that is between each individual and God. We can't set our standards by the actions of other people, even if they are *truly* Christians, because human beings *will* let you down if given enough time; this is why we must make Jesus and the Word of God our focal point – not any man or woman. Romans 3:23 says, 'For all have sinned, and come short of the glory of God;' This means even if you set your standards on the most righteous man or woman on earth, they will fall short, and so will you."

"So the only way to heaven is through faith in Jesus, and him only." Tim stated in a questioning manner.

"Yes." I answered. "Just like I quoted on Wednesday, John 14:6 says, 'Jesus saith unto him, I am the way, the truth, and the life: no man cometh unto the Father, but by me.' This keeps things simple and to the point, otherwise, confusion is inevitable."

"Ok, that leads me to another question, and this one might be a little tough." He said, as he searched for a way to put his thoughts into words. "If there is no way to heaven except through Jesus….what happens to someone who is born in some remote area of the world, and is never told anything about the Bible or Jesus?"

"That is a very good question Tim. There are a lot of people wrestling with that, and other similar questions." I wasn't sure exactly how to approach this one, because there are so many different avenues that could be taken. I had pondered on this very thought so many times in my own past, and I had come to a peaceful understanding, however, I didn't want to confuse them with a poor outline of the subject; I wanted to keep things in a simple, yet thorough order.

"I want to start by saying that God is in charge of everything, and he can do whatever he wants; as I said before, it is only by his grace that *any* of us are saved, however, I'm going to tell you what the Bible says, and there is a lot of scripture to go over here so let me know if I get off task, and start losing you."

They both nodded their heads.

"Knowledge plays a key role in the answer to this question, and I'm going to show you that even if someone has never '*heard*' of Jesus Christ, they are still accountable to God, because we all know– whether we admit it or not – that there is a God who created us, and his laws are written in our hearts. I read part of this to you earlier, but I'm going to add a couple of verses to it. Romans 1:18-22 says, 'For the wrath of God is revealed from heaven against all ungodliness and unrighteousness of men, who hold the truth in unrighteousness; Because that which may be known of God is manifest in them; for God hath showed it unto them; For the invisible things of him from the creation of the world are clearly seen, being understood by the things that are made, even his eternal power and Godhead; so that they are without excuse.' This tells that God has manifested in us exactly what he wants us to know, and no one can look at everything around them, and come to the conclusion that there is no God – no matter what corner of the world their standing in. Romans 12:3 tells about how each of us is also given faith….it says, 'For I say, through the grace given unto me, to every man that is among you, not to think of himself more highly than he ought to think; but to think soberly, according as God hath dealt to every man the measure of faith.'"

I could see that Carmen seemed to be following me so far, and Tim also appeared to be engaged. I think Carmen was happy that she understood the Bible verses better than she'd previously thought, and she enjoyed commenting on them.

"That makes sense," She explained. "That measure of faith, and manifested knowledge you mentioned would explain why everyone seems to be looking for God at some point in their lives – even if they choose to ignore what they know in their hearts."

"That's right," I answered. "God has embedded this in all of us, in order for us to seek him, but we have the ability to suppress that knowledge; if you think about it, those godly men and women of the Old Testament had never had the gospel of Jesus Christ preached to them, but they knew in their hearts that God was real, and they chose to follow him – many were even spoken to by God, and I sincerely believe that God has many ways of revealing himself to those who will accept him and seek him even today. We have to remember that God knows everyone's heart, and he knows whether or not they will accept him or not, so he is under no obligation to give anyone anymore information than is already available to them, however, if there *is* someone in a remote area of the world that is seeking the truth, God will use whatever means necessary to draw them to him – believe me, God knows where everyone is, because he placed them there as it says in Acts 17:26-27, 'And hath made of one blood all nations of men for to dwell on all the face of the earth, and hath determined the times before appointed, and the bounds of their habitation; That they should seek the Lord, if haply they might feel after him, and find him, though he be not far from every one of us:'"

"I guess he knows that there are some people who will not follow him no matter what he reveals to them." Carmen added.

"Very true." I said as I nodded my head in agreement. "Even when Jesus walked the earth, performing miracle after miracle, there were still people who chose not to believe, and there has always been people – just like today – who are offended by the truth; now they probably wish they had chosen a different path, but it is too late for them."

"What did you mean when you said God's law was in our hearts?" Tim asked.

"Well, that is another way that God has revealed himself to everyone, and it's known as your ability to discern right and wrong coupled with your conscience. Our minds, and our brains are different all together, which, attests to the fact that we are not just physical bodies walking around – we have a soul that will live on after death, and our conscience has been deeply embedded in all of us by God. Romans 2:14-15 says, 'For when the Gentiles, which have not the law, do by nature the things contained in the law, these, having not the law, are a law unto themselves: Which show the work of the law written in their hearts, their conscience also bearing witness, and their thoughts the mean while accusing or excusing one another;' This tells about people doing the right things by nature, because God's law is in there hearts….just like you and I know what's right and wrong, and make our choices accordingly. If our actions were controlled only by physical matter known as the brain, it would be hard to hold people accountable for wrong doings since the brain functions in ways that we have no control over, but since our mind is what makes us all individual and unique, we are able to choose what our brain commands our body to do."

"Is that the knowledge you were talking about?" Carmen asked.

"That's definitely part of it. Those are the things that God has given to all of us, so that everyone has a chance to know him; depending on each individual's circumstances the amount of knowledge above and beyond this will vary, and God knows what each person will be accountable for; mankind is responsible for what we know, and God's revelation has been progressive since the beginning of time, so all that is needed is faith in what the Lord has revealed to us. Proverbs 24:12 says, 'If thou sayest, behold, we knew it not; doth not he that pondereth the heart consider it? And he that keepeth thy soul, doth not he know it? And shall not he render to every man according to his works?' This tells how God is aware of what we *know* and what we *don't know*; then James 4:17 says, 'Therefore to him that knoweth to do good, and doeth it not, to him it is sin.' And Romans 5:13 says, 'For until the law sin was in the world: but sin is not imputed when there is no law.' These two verses show that sin is imputed based on the knowledge available."

"That makes me feel better about God's justice;" Carmen stated, with a sigh of relief. "He's not going to punish someone for something they knew nothing about, but ignoring things that they *know* in their heart is true, won't get them off the hook, because everyone knows God's laws."

"Very well put." I said, with a smile, and I must say that I was very proud of the progress these two had made. "One thing we can all count on is God's justice; Genesis 18:25 says, 'That be far from thee to do after this manner, to slay the righteous with the wicked: and that the righteous should be as the wicked, that be far from thee: Shall not the judge of all the earth do right?'"

"What does God say about non-believers who were good people? Do they get the same punishment as a mass murderer?" Tim asked.

"To answer that you have to understand that there are different degrees of punishment, just like there are different degrees of reward for the faithful." I answered. "No non-believer will be taken to heaven no matter how good they were, but there are several scriptures that allude to different punishments based on their works. In Mathew 10:14-15 Jesus says to his disciples, 'And whosoever shall not receive you, nor hear your words, when ye depart out of that house or city, shake off the dust of your feet. Verily I say unto you, It shall be more tolerable for the land of Sodom and Gomorrha in the day of judgment, than for that city.' Then another verse is 2 Peter 2:20-21 which says, 'For if after they have escaped the pollutions of the world through the knowledge of the Lord and Savior Jesus Christ, they are again entangled therein, and overcome, the latter end is worse with them than the beginning. For it had been better for them not to have known the way of righteousness, than, after they have known it, to turn from the holy commandment delivered unto them.' This emphasizes again, that when you know to do right and don't, there's a heavier price. I don't fully understand myself the implications of varying degrees of punishment because scripture doesn't really elaborate comprehensively on this topic, and there is never a pleasant picture of Hell no matter how you look at is so all in all this is in God's hands."

I could tell Tim's mind was working overtime again as he started to speak.

"What about believers who were alive before Jesus was born, were they saved too?" He asked.

"They were saved, and they were saved by the blood of Jesus; you have to remember what I said earlier, about God, Jesus, and the Holy Spirit being one, and they have all been around from the beginning, even though the people in the Old Testament had never seen Jesus. The difference between the Old Testament men and women, and those that came after the resurrection, is that no one could be with God in eternity without justification, and complete forgiveness of all sin, which came when Jesus died and was resurrected; those who died before went to a place called *sheol,* also referred to as Hades, which contained both the wicked and the good, but it was divided into two distinct places with a great gulf fixed between them that no one could cross – Abraham's bosom and hell. Luke chapter 16:19-31 tells the story of Lazarus, who was a beggar, and the rich man who wouldn't even feed Lazarus with the crumbs that fell from his table; as the story goes on, they both died and the angels carried Lazarus to Abraham's bosom to be comforted, but the rich man opened his eyes in hell, being tormented."

"So what happened to those that were in Sheol after Jesus was resurrected?" He asked.

"After the resurrection, the sin debt was paid in full, so they were taken to Heaven as described in Ephesians 4:8-9 which says, 'Wherefore he saith, When he ascended up on high, he led captivity captive, and gave gifts unto men. Now that he ascended, what is it but that he also descended first into the lower parts of the earth.' Leading captivity captive is taking those who were captive in Hades. When a person who is saved dies today, their spirit is taken directly to the Lord as it says in 2 Corinthians 5:6-9 'Therefore we are always confident, knowing that, whilst we are at home in the body, we are absent from the Lord: For we walk by faith, not by sight: We are confident, I say, and willing rather to be absent from the body, and to be present with the Lord.' This means that as soon as our spirit is absent from the body, we are present with the Lord."

"I always thought Hades was another word for Hell, but I guess I was just miss-informed." Tim said, staring at the floor, obviously thinking back to his previous beliefs. "What your saying makes sense, and the pieces of the puzzle fit together just as they should. There really does seem to be an answer for everything if you know where to look."

"The Bible has everything we need, and many have spent their whole lives studying it, only to find out that everyday is another chance to learn even more. I want to add one more thing in order to sum up this topic – God doesn't want anyone to suffer an eternity in Hell, as Ezekiel 18:32, and 2 Peter 3:9 state, 'For I have no pleasure in the death of him that dieth, saith the Lord God: wherefore turn yourselves, and live ye. The Lord is not slack concerning his promise, as some men count slackness; but is long-suffering to us-ward, not willing that any should perish, but that all should come to repentance.' God *knows* who will accept him – he doesn't want anyone to perish – he doesn't *forget* about anyone – he is *just*, and he will reach everyone no matter how obscure their location is in this world; even people indoctrinated with false religions will find God if they genuinely search for the truth, but if they just go with whatever people tell them and ignore what their conscience tells them, they will remain lost. Did that answer your question well enough?" I asked.

"It did." Tim responded. "I figured that one would be a lot harder for you." He said smiling.

"It does sound like an un-answerable question, but when the facts are lined up, it doesn't prove to be that hard." I said.

Carmen was seemingly anxious to jump in again, so I give her a gesture to go ahead.

"Since knowledge plays a key role in what we're responsible for, does that mean children, and mentally impaired people who die are automatically saved?" She asked.

"That's a good question, and it happens to be one that the Bible doesn't directly address by specifically mentioning what happens when a child or a mentally impaired person dies, however, have either of you heard of the age of accountability?"

They both shook their heads.

"The age of accountability is a concept that has been adopted by most Christians, based mainly on the scriptures in 2 Samuel chapters 11 and 12, which describe how King David, who was a man of God, had an affair with the wife of one of his soldiers, who became pregnant; David sent this soldier to the front lines of the battle so he would be killed, in order for him to take Bath-sheba as his wife, and therefore cover up the affair. God sent a man to David, telling him that because of his sin, the child would die, and sure enough the child became very sick – eventually dying. David sorrowed for the child up until the baby's death, and then the grieving abruptly stopped, which brought on questions from his servants. In 2 Samuel 12:22-23 David replies to them, 'And he said, while the child was yet alive, I fasted and wept: for I said, who can tell whether God will be gracious to me, that the child may live? But now he is dead, wherefore should I fast? Can I bring him back again? I shall go to him, but he shall not return to me.' David acknowledges that the child is gone, but he can go to the child; since David, even though sinful, had faith in God and believed he would be reunited with his son in heaven. The child had not reached an age where he would understand his need for a savior, and thus didn't have the ability to make a choice *for* or *against* God; the same would hold true for a person who doesn't have the mental ability to make this choice, however, if someone became mentally impaired *after* reaching the age of accountability, due to some type of accident or something, then they *would* be held accountable for not accepting Jesus Christ when they had the chance. As I said before, the Bible doesn't specifically address these two scenario's, but we do know that whatever God does will be *just,* and 1 John 2:1-2 says, 'My little children, these things write I unto you, that ye sin not. And if any man sin, we have an advocate with the Father, Jesus Christ the righteous: And he is the propitiation for our sins: and not for ours only, but also for the sins of the whole world.' This tells me that the death of Jesus Christ was enough to cover all of our sin debts, even the little ones."

"Even though the Bible doesn't say that, it does sound logical that a merciful God would handle things that way." Carmen added.

"I would agree with that too." Tim stated, nodding his head. "It would be a shame for God to punish the smallest of his creations, when they haven't even had the opportunity to reject him."

"Since we've mentioned mercy and handicaps," Carmen added, as she contemplated her next question. "Why would a merciful God allow people to be born into bad situations, such as: abusive environments, starvation, or even handicaps?"

"I think we've all wondered that at some time or another." I replied, searching for a good answer to this timeless question. "Ever since the fall of man, when death entered into the picture, we as human beings became vulnerable to all sorts of ailments, deformities, and so on. Sometimes mental illnesses, sicknesses, and deformities are a direct result of bad choices made by the parents such as: drug abuse, drinking or smoking during the pregnancy, along with countless other possibilities, and then sometimes there just doesn't seem to be a logical reason for these things. The fact is that bad things happen to good people and bad people alike, and sometimes at the hands of an evil person, so it begs the question – how could God allow this to happen? There are *way* too many possibilities to cover here, so I'm just going to throw a few things out there for you to think about. I'm sure you've both heard the expression, 'when life gives you lemons – make lemonade.' Haven't you?"

They both acknowledged hearing this by nodding their heads.

"No one goes through life without problems, even if some appear to have it made. Until you've walked a mile in their shoes – so to speak – you really can't know what pain and disappointment they may be hiding from everyone. As it says in Job 14:1 'Man that is born of a woman is of few days, and full of trouble' however, those who have put their trust in God, have help in times of trouble. Psalm 55:22 says 'Cast thy burden upon the Lord, and he shall sustain thee: he shall never suffer the righteous to be moved.' Those who believe, and have an active relationship with the Lord, can take their burdens to him, and if they are willing to listen, there very well could be a blessing waiting for them – even in the midst of a somewhat bad situation, and there's always an opportunity to extol the Lord by our responses to these situations. Did you kids know that Moses had a speech impediment?"

"I've never heard that." Carmen replied, and Tim was shaking his head.

"Moses is a good example of what God can do with something that we consider a handicap. The book of Exodus tells the story of Moses, and in chapter 4 verses 10-12, it says, 'And Moses said unto the Lord, O my Lord, I am not eloquent, neither heretofore, nor since thou hast spoken unto thy servant: but I am slow of speech, and of a slow tongue. And the Lord said unto him, Who hath made man's mouth? Or who maketh the dumb, or deaf, or the seeing, or the blind? Have not I the Lord? Now therefore go, and I will be with thy mouth, and teach thee what thou shalt say.' this shows how God wanted to use his speech problem, and Moses went on to be a great leader, because he trusted and followed God. Anything that happens – good or bad – happens because God allows it to for his own reasons, and the outcome is something that only he knows, so we shouldn't question it; we should only pray to God that he would reveal to us what he wants us to do with the life we're given; a Christian needs to live above circumstances in order for them to realize God's plan. One thing is for sure, and that is when we humble ourselves to God, and allow him to guide us into the life that he wants for us....we will experience true peace, and happiness. That gives you an idea of how God can use a handicap, and now I'll give you a scenario that shows one possible reason why someone may be born into a bad situation, and please remember that this is only one possible example; I am in *no way* saying that I know for sure this is God's plan in a situation like this, and I'm sure there are many different reasons for something like this. Let's say you have Bill over here, who has been physically abused all his life by his alcoholic father, however, he has chosen to seek God in the midst of the turmoil; he gets saved, eventually grows up, and gets out on his own. Now because of his active relationship with God, he is able to forgive his father, and God helps him cope with the mental wounds he has accumulated. Now over in the other corner we have Joe, who has *also* grown up being abused by an alcoholic father, but Joe has refused God's draw, and has decided to let anger rule his life, which has landed him in prison for murder. Are you with me so far?"

"I think so." Carmen answered. "You're describing how free will has allowed one person to make a bad situation better by accepting God, and the other person has made a bad situation worse by refusing God."

"Sounds like you're following quite well." I said smiling, and then my attention was drawn to Tim, who obviously had something to add.

"I'm also following you so far," he said, "but I still don't understand why either one of them had to be born into that type of situation in the first place."

"Well, that's my next point." I replied. "All the troubles we experience in this life have been the consequences of sin. God warns us against sin but we do it anyway and then complain when the price has to be paid. In this case their fathers made the sinful choice of abuse, which put the children in that situation, and ultimately they will have to answer for that; Ephesians 6:4 says, 'And, ye fathers, provoke not your children to wrath: but bring them up in the nurture and admonition of the Lord.' Now, just because they placed a terrible burden on their son's, doesn't mean that God can't use this for his purposes; if he allowed it to happen, then there must be a reason for it."

"You've lost me on that one." Carmen said. "Those kids will be living with that for the rest of their lives, so I'm not sure what *good* can come of it."

"I know it's hard to grasp, but you have to remember....we cannot see the big picture, and therefore have no insight into the outcome; you see, a person like Joe, who has lived a life full of rage, is very hard to connect with by anyone trying to help him, and God knows this, so who do you think would have a better chance witnessing to Joe...someone pretending to understand his painful experiences, or someone like Bill who knows exactly what he has gone through, and has prevailed?"

I looked at both of them, trying to decipher their expressions, and I could almost see the wheels of their minds turning as they manipulated the different possibilities of this situation.

"I'm with you now." She said, nodding. "It's hard to see the possibility of a good result, when you're so focused on the bad."

"That's very true, and I'm reminded of Romans 8:28, which should help us all to trust God's sovereignty; it says, 'And we know that all things work together for good to them that love God, to them who are the called according to his purpose.' Since Bill has given his life to the Lord, it would be very easy for God to lead him into a prison ministry or something that would bring him into contact with Joe, because as I said earlier, God doesn't want anyone to go to hell. This type of scenario would also hold true for those with handicaps, as well as, other ailments and afflictions, because there is a common ground that makes witnessing more effective. Another thing to think about is the fact that people sometimes seem to be more receptive to God when they're hurting in some way, so if God has to allow a bad situation to take place in order to get through to them, then so be it."

"I guess someone who doesn't follow God can't expect things to always work out to their benefit as well can they?" Tim added.

"God knows what all of us are in need of, and he will take care of those who love him, but he also knows who will accept him farther on down the road, so I'm sure he'll do what is necessary for them to reach that point, even if it takes something painful to get their attention. There are many tragedies happening around the world all the time, and people wonder how God could let something like that happen....some even assume that people are being punished for something they've done, but we don't know that for sure; God could be punishing some, and getting the attention of others. We just have to accept the fact that God knows what he's doing, and he doesn't need our help or input."

"I hope those who do suffer here on earth will be rewarded for it." Carmen said inquisitively.

"If they've accepted Jesus Christ, there will be rewards for their suffering. Many Christians go through life dealing with all sorts of pain, and suffering, and even persecutions because of their faith, but Psalm 22:24 says, 'For he hath not despised nor abhorred the affliction of the afflicted; neither hath he hid his face from him; but when he cried unto him, he heard.' And Psalm 126:5-6 says, 'They that sow in tears shall reap in joy. He that goeth forth and weepeth, bearing precious seed, shall doubtless come again with rejoicing, bringing his sheaves with him.' God knows our afflictions, and there will be joy for those who continue sowing the seeds in the midst of pain and suffering; it is also the duty of those who are not afflicted, to do what we can to help our fellow man with the ultimate goal of glorifying the Lord and leading others to him. Sometimes the waters are going to get a little rough, but no one can become a good captain unless they know how to navigate through a storm."

"It was always hard for me to believe that God was real, since he didn't seem to stop his followers from being harmed by evil people." Tim said staring at the floor. "I remember seeing an interview one time of a girl who had been brutally raped, and subsequently became pregnant, but she continued to exclaim her faith in God's plan, and insisted on going through with the pregnancy. I thought to myself that she had to be delusional for continuing to believe in a God that didn't protect her from this, and I couldn't see why anyone would want to have a baby fathered by their attacker, but things look a little different now, and I'm sure God could use her situation too."

"That's exactly right Tim." I said. "That is another question that comes up a lot, and some use it as an excuse to terminate the pregnancy, but abortion is *never ever* excusable. That man did an extremely terrible thing of his own free will, and should be punished for it, but the child that is developing in the womb is innocent. Some think that the child would be a constant reminder to the mother, and should be terminated, but I have news for them – that mother will always have that attack buried within her mind, and it is not going to help her at all to add the thought of knowing that she killed an innocent unborn child as an attempt to clear her mind. That is a terrible, evil situation, and I feel for anyone who goes through something like that, because it must be awful, but God allowed her to get pregnant and will help her deal with the trauma if she will only go to him, and who knows, that child may grow up to be a blessing to humanity, and she has the opportunity to emerge stronger than before, if her heart is right. No one is saying she has to keep the baby either; there are many couples out there who would love to adopt that child into their family if the mother doesn't feel like she's up to it. I'm reminded of a country song I heard many years ago titled 'Three wooden crosses' which is a story about a farmer, a preacher, a hooker, and a teacher, that were riding on the same bus, and ended up in a bad accident. There were three of the four killed in the accident, and the song leads you to believe that the preacher was the only survivor, but in actuality it was the hooker that survived; most people hearing this song for the first time are thinking, how could God let the preacher die, and save the hooker….this is also an example of bad things happening to a good person, but the end of the song holds the answer to that question. The preacher handed his blood stained Bible to the hooker just before he passed away, and God used this experience to change her life. In essence, the preacher who is telling this story to his congregation one Sunday morning is the son of the hooker, and now follows God, because she read it to him as he was growing up. It's hard to look at death as a good thing, but think about it this way….the preacher was able to do one last thing for his savior just before he died and is now getting his reward in heaven, but if it had been the other way around, the hooker would be tormented in hell for her rejection of God; since God used the preacher's death to reach her, she and her son are better off."

By the look on Tim's face, things were starting to really sink in and take root in his mind – maybe now his thought process will forever be changed in a good way, however, it did appear that something was still troubling him though.

"I guess that re-enforces the fact that we all have to trust that God is in control – no matter how grim the circumstances, because fighting it will only bury us in self pity, and forbid us from seeing our purpose in life." He said, still staring at the porch floor.

"I understand the points of those stories, but I've got one question about the Bill, and Joe story. I don't see how Bill could just forgive his father so easily."

"Why do you say that?" I asked.

"Well, I know someone who was a victim of abuse, and hearing about some of the things she went through makes me so angry that I want to really hurt the man responsible. I can't imagine how much worse it must be for her, and I don't see how forgiveness would be possible."

I could tell that Tim was very emotional about this subject, and for the first time during our conversation there was anger in his eyes – obviously brought on by the thought of forgiving someone who seemingly does not deserve it.

"I know how you feel Tim," I explained. "Because I know people in this type of situation, and believe me, forgiveness is never easy, and sometimes forgiveness seems impossible, but nothing is impossible with God, and once a person is saved, the power of forgiveness is ours through prayer, obedience to God, and the work of the Holy Spirit in our lives. Some situations are so bad that *only* through a relationship with God, can true forgiveness be reached. Many times forgiveness is more important for the *forgiver*, than it is for the one being *forgiven,* because holding on to grudges or hatred is like jumping in a lake with an anchor tied around your neck; no matter how hard you try to swim towards the surface, you will continue to sink, because of the weight that holds you down. There is a real blessing awaiting those who are willing to forgive, because it will release them from the chains of anger, and hatred that is dragging them down. Jesus said in Mathew 5:44-47, 'But I say unto you, love your enemies, bless them that curse you, do good to them that hate you, and pray for them which despitefully use you, and persecute you; That ye may be the children of your Father which is in heaven: for he maketh his sun to rise on the evil and on the good, and sendeth rain on the just and on the unjust. For if ye love them which love you, what reward have ye? Do not even the publicans the same? And if ye salute your brethren only, what do ye more than others? Do not even the publicans so?' Anyone can show love and forgiveness to their brethren, but a Christian is to go a step further, and God gives us the ability to do that if we are willing to follow his lead. One thing you don't want to do is confuse forgiveness and trust, which are two entirely different things; you can forgive someone of something they've done, without necessarily trusting them, because trust has to be earned, and that will take time."

"I guess that's something that I would just have to experience in order to understand; I've never had that relationship you're talking about, so it seems out of reach." He said.

Carmen was gently rubbing his shoulders in a gesture of understanding.

She then turned to me and said, "Is there anything that *is* unforgivable – against us....or God?"

"When Jesus died on the cross, his blood was sufficient to pay the price for all sins that *had* been committed – all sins that *were being* committed, and all sins that *will be* committed, however, it is a gift that must be accepted, in order to be applied to anyone's sin debt; what this means is, no matter how great your sins are, there is forgiveness available unless you choose to reject God. Mark 3:28-29 talks about the response Jesus made to the scribes from Jerusalem, who kept rejecting the validity of Jesus being the Son of God, and they even accused him of having a demon. In these verses it says, 'Verily I say unto you, all sins shall be forgiven unto the sons of men, and blasphemies where-with soever they shall blaspheme; But he that shall blaspheme against the Holy Ghost hath never forgiveness, but is in danger of eternal damnation.' So to answer your question – the only unforgivable sin to God is rejection, and that is because he is merciful; if you decide to start a relationship with the Lord, you will find that he is willing to risk, forgive, and show mercy in a way far beyond what we would do if in his position."

"Since he created us, I would say that's reasonable." Carmen added. "I always thought the God of Christianity expected perfection from us, but it seems he only wants us to believe and put our trust in him, and be obedient."

"Very well put." I said. "And just a little comment on perfection – we should all try to live like Jesus who *is* perfect, and even though we will never measure up to him....it should always be our goal."

"What about limitations on forgiving other people?" Tim asked.

"Well, Mathew 6:14 says, 'For if ye forgive men their trespasses, your heavenly Father will also forgive you:' And Luke 6:35-38 says, 'But love ye your enemies, and do good, and lend, hoping for nothing again; and your reward shall be great, and ye shall be the children of the Highest: for he is kind unto the unthankful and to the evil. Be ye therefore merciful, as your Father also is merciful. Judge not, and ye shall not be judged: condemn not, and ye shall not be condemned: forgive, and ye shall be forgiven: Give, and it shall be given unto you; good measure, pressed down, and shaken together, and running over shall men give into your bosom. For with the same measure that ye mete withal it shall be measured to you again.' So it seems that forgiveness is in a Christian's best interest, and the reward will be great; however, a Christian's duty is to offer forgiveness to those who are in need of it; it doesn't mean they will feel the need to be forgiven, or that they will be willing to repent from their transgressions, and accept it. Jesus explains this in Luke 17:1-4 which says, 'Then said he unto the disciples, It is impossible but that offenses will come: but woe unto him, through whom they come! It were better for him that a millstone were hanged about his neck, and he cast into the sea, than that he should offend one of these little ones. Take heed to yourselves: If thy brother trespass against thee, rebuke him; and if he repent, forgive him. And if he trespass against thee seven times in a day, and seven times in a day turn again to thee, saying, I repent; thou shalt forgive him.'"

"So they must be willing to change their ways?" Tim inquired.

"That's right." I said. "To repent is to turn away from, and have a change of heart, which some people are not willing to do, and if they don't…. we have done all that we can do by offering our forgiveness, and our conscience can be clear."

"I know you're probably ready to move on," Carmen said, hesitantly. "But since we're talking about forgiveness, I have a friend who claims that as a so called 'Christian nation,' we shouldn't be involved in a war, because we are supposed to forgive those people who attacked us. What is your opinion on that?"

"I have heard that one too." I said, rolling my eyes in disgust. "Many of the people who use that one are anti-war, and sometimes, anti-God; they are trying to find a way to use the Bible to further their cause, even though they don't really believe it, however, there are also some true Christians out there, who are just a little confused on the forgiveness topic. Ecclesiastes 3:1-8 is a good passage to start answering this question; it says, 'To every thing there is a season, and a time to every purpose under the heaven: A time to be born, and a time to die; a time to plant, and a time to pluck up that which is planted; A time to kill, and a time to heal; a time to break down, and a time to build up; A time to weep, and a time to laugh; a time to mourn, and a time to dance; A time to cast away stones, and a time to gather stones together; a time to embrace, and a time to refrain from embracing; A time to get, and a time to lose; a time to keep, and a time to cast away; A time to rend, and a time to sew; a time to keep silence, and a time to speak; A time to love, and a time to hate; a time of war, and a time of peace.' This clearly states that there *is* a time for war, so can either one of you think of a reason for our country to be at war right now, instead of just forgiving those who attacked us?" I asked.

They both sat in silence for a few moments then I could see enlightenment spread across Tim's face in the form of a smile.

"Actually you answered that a moment ago when you answered my last question." He said. "The people who attacked us are not remorseful, and they do not believe they've done anything wrong due to their twisted religious beliefs, so therefore they are not willing to repent, and they are not going to ask forgiveness; they believe that the annihilation of the United States is what their God wants them to do."

"Bingo." I said smiling with the same expression a proud parent would have when their child has done something extraordinary. "When dealing with someone who is focused on killing you, it is necessary to defend yourself, and you can't forgive someone if they don't want it, but we should pray for them that they will someday realize the error of their ways, and begin searching for the true and living God; did you kids know that there was actually war in Heaven at one time?"

"That's a new one on me." Tim said surprised, and Carmen looked a little bewildered, as she shook her head.

"Remember earlier when we were talking about Satan, and his angels, and I read you a passage about the dragon's tail sweeping a third of the stars out of heaven?"

They both nodded as they recollected the story.

"The verses I read are in Revelation chapter 12, and if you continue reading in verses 7-9 it says, 'And there was war in heaven: Michael and his angels fought against the dragon; and the dragon fought and his angels, and prevailed not; neither was their place found any more in heaven. And the great dragon was cast out, that old serpent, called the Devil, and Satan, which deceiveth the whole world: he was cast out into the earth, and his angels were cast out with him.' So war is sometimes unavoidable, because *someone* or *some group* you cannot control makes the choice to stand for evil, and therefore you must defend yourself."

"There must be a lot of confusion about what Christians are supposed to do, and what their not supposed to do." Carmen said.

"Why do you say that?" I asked.

"Well, many people – like my friend – claim to be Christians, but they can't seem to agree on very much; just like the war question, there are many other things that everyone seems to have a different answer for, and there are some who do terrible things that they claim was in the name of God."

"There *is* a lot of confusion among Christians, and the reason for most of this confusion is simply that people are not doing what God has instructed us to do. The Bible states very plainly that we are to study God's word – meditate on it daily, and pray diligently, so that the Lord can guide us down the right path, and expose the un-truth's that are lurking around every corner. When Christians don't do this, or if their study treats individual verses as stand-alone instruction instead of paying close attention to context, they leave themselves open to suggestion, as well as, anything else Satan can come up with. This takes me back to something I mentioned before – not everyone who *claims* to be a Christian *is* a Christian; remember earlier when I quoted some verses in Mathew chapter 7, which talked about how not everyone who says Lord, Lord will enter into Heaven, even though there would be those who claim to have done great things in the name of the Lord?"

They both nodded their heads.

"This is a perfect example of some of the so called preachers, and disciples that stand in front of very large numbers of people today spreading lies, and deceit; since the majority of these people don't study the Bible for themselves, they believe what they hear, and end up continuing the spread of these lies in their daily conversations – if we don't study the Bible – we won't know if what's being preached is true. There are even people out there who *enjoy* diluting the pureness of Christianity by doing evil things, and saying God told them too, because they know that their actions will inevitably cause someone to reject Christianity. These are not the only reasons people do these things by no means, but no matter what the circumstances are, Satan will try to use them to further his agenda."

"I've noticed that it always seems to be Christianity that is attacked in this way." Tim added observantly. "Every time there's some nut job who convinces their congregation that the world is going to end on a certain day, and then leads them into a mass suicide or something, it's always portrayed as a Christian group, and it always made me think to myself that there's no way I could believe any religion, because the actions of those people created a stereotypical image in my mind of all believers. I guess there are a lot of people out there who have turned their backs on religion, because of this type of thing. I also wondered why it seemed that only things relating to Christianity were being questioned in our government – you know how they want everything to do with God taken out of the public eye."

"That's a very good observation." I commended him. "And the reason Christianity gets attacked like this is because Satan is not worried about all the false religions out there – they're no threat to him; he is only worried about dismantling the truth, and this is why it is so crucial for true believers to get out there and evangelize by spreading the true gospel of Jesus Christ to those who are lost, before Satan is able to deceive them. Most of these other religions out there don't teach just one way to their God; many even have multiple God's, and they feel that anything can be true as long as you sincerely believe it, so it's your choice as to what religion suits your way of living better. Christianity, on the other hand, doesn't pretend that it's all about you and you can have it your way; it clearly states one God – one way to God – and this is what God wants from us. There is no reason to attack something unless you feel threatened by it. Satan is threatened by Christianity, so he has his people working overtime to try and destroy its legitimacy. There are attacks on other religions as well, which I believe is a ploy by Satan to place all religions on the same playing field, and instigate the rejection of all religious beliefs, but the biggest attacks are on Christianity. Your story reminded me of Deuteronomy 18:22 which says, 'When a prophet speaketh in the name of the Lord, if the thing follow not, nor come to pass, that is the thing which the Lord hath not spoken, but the prophet hath spoken it presumptuously: thou shalt not be afraid of him.' True disciples of Jesus Christ are able to discern between these false prophets, and the real thing, because of the witness of the Holy Spirit, but unfortunately there are a lot of false disciples out there too. Jesus talks about what is necessary to be a disciple in Luke 14:26 which says, 'If any man come to me, and hate not his father, and mother, and wife, and children, and brethren, and sisters, yea, and his own life also, he cannot be my disciple.'"

I noticed the look of complete confusion on both of their faces, which is exactly the reaction I'd hoped for when I chose to quote this verse.

"Ok – maybe I misunderstood what you just said," Tim explained. "But that sounded like we were being ordered to hate our families, and friends, in order to follow Jesus."

"I'm very confused also." Carmen weighed in. "I thought Jesus taught *love* not *hate.*"

"I was hoping you kids wouldn't let that one slip by you." I said proudly. "The reason I chose this verse was not only to describe what Jesus requires of his disciples, but to also give an example of a verse that non-believers will take out of context, and use it as an example of Biblical contradiction."

"I take it your saying this is not a contradiction to his teachings of love." Carmen inquired.

"Definitely not." I answered. "Jesus teaches us to love one another, and to honor our parents, so what exactly do you think this verse means?"

"I have no idea, but I'm assuming that context has something to do with this." Tim replied.

"Very good." I complimented him. "Context is the answer to this, and when this passage is examined thoroughly, you will find that Jesus was merely explaining the cost to someone that has decided to follow him. He's not telling them to *literally* hate themselves, and everyone around them, but instead he is using this wording to show them that to be his disciple will take no less than *absolute dedication* – meaning that family, friends, and even themselves will have to be secondary compared to their devotion to him – your love for your parents should seem like hate compared to your love for Jesus. Sometimes a Christian's love for Jesus will cause those who are close to him or her, but not sharing the same belief, to turn against him or her – dividing family and friends. There's another scripture that compliments this very well, which is Mathew 10:34-39; Jesus says, 'Think not that I am come to send peace on earth: I came not to send peace, but a sword. For I am come to set a man at variance against his father, and the daughter against her mother, and the daughter-in-law against her mother-in-law. And a man's foes shall be they of his own household. He that loveth father or mother more than me is not worthy of me: and he that loveth son or daughter more than me is not worthy of me. And he that taketh not his cross, and followeth after me, is not worthy of me. He that findeth his life shall lose it: and he that loseth his life for my sake shall find it."

"Ok, I see what you're saying." Carmen's eyes lit up with understanding once more. "He's basically telling them that the focal point of their lives must be centered around him in order to do his will, and it's being brought across as a comparative to hatred; I'm guessing this is, because, if people are not focusing on him they will be out doing their own will, and not his."

"Bravo." I commended her while giving the ceremonial clap of my hands.

Just as I finished clapping my hands, our attention was drawn to the ring of Tim's cell phone. As he answered, and began speaking to the other party I couldn't help but feel a little sad, because this was a call that I had been dreading for some time now. It would mean that my time with these two wonderful people was coming to a close, and I would very soon be like the parent who watches their teenager leave for college – I would have to let them go, and put my faith in Jesus to take it from here.

"Well, they've got my jeep finished, and said we could pick it up whenever we're ready….as long as it's before five." He said solemnly. It was obvious that he was a little disappointed in our time coming to a close also.

"It's only three o'clock now so that gives us a little more time to talk." Carmen added. "That is if you don't mind Jack"

"Of course I don't." I said, more than happy to re-engage. "I'll take you there whenever you're ready."

Chapter 9
Wrapping things up

"Now that we've only got a couple of hours left, it's hard to decide what needs to be asked." Carmen said.

"That always seems to happen when time is an issue." I responded, "But at least you now have a foundation to build on, in order to find answers for yourselves in the future."

"That's true, but you have so much more experience with this, and I'm afraid that I don't quite trust my understanding of the Bible enough to be comfortable yet." She said hesitantly.

"No one is perfect Carmen, and no one starts out, or finishes life understanding everything; we all have to start at the bottom, and work our way through our relationship with God. All you need to do is believe, and put your trust in Jesus Christ, then he will guide you; remember what I said about equating being born again with starting out as a child in the family of God?"

She nodded.

"Once you've given your life to Christ you will receive the Holy Spirit, and he will be your teacher. Read your Bible every day, and God will speak to you, and teach you from his word; believe me it is a wonderful experience as you start learning, and things that didn't make sense before all of a sudden become clear as crystal. Proverbs 1:23 says, 'Turn you at my reproof: behold, I will pour out my spirit unto you, I will make known my words unto you.' One thing you have to keep in mind is that you have to work at this relationship just as you would a human relationship or it will not grow. It pains me to think about people who say they've given up on God, because he doesn't answer their prayers, or maybe they don't feel his presence in their lives, but they fail to put two and two together, realizing that they have no relationship with him. I've seen these people myself living a life that in *no way* even resembles a Godly life, but as soon as a little trouble crosses their path, they decide to pray for help, and then seem confused by the fact that there's no answer. If a person truly loves God then they will want to obey his laws, and live a life accordingly, otherwise, they are just looking for a deity to help them out of trouble when they need it, and leave them alone to pursue their sins when things are going good for them. This leads me to believe that maybe they're not really saved in the first place, since there's no desire to follow God."

"How do you know if you actually get saved?" She asked.

"That question is very simple, but over the years man has gotten involved, and created much confusion, and unfortunately many false converts. Some will tell you that if you just say this certain prayer, and ask Jesus into your heart your saved; even though it *is* possible to be saved by praying in a way that is similar to their example prayer, people have to realize that unless God is drawing them, and they're speaking sincerely from their heart, these are merely words. The reality is – *they can't save you, and they can't tell you that you're saved!* You will know without a shadow of a doubt when the Lord is drawing you, because it will feel as though your heart is being pulled out of your chest; you will be restless, and in your heart you will know that you are in need of salvation; in other words you will understand that you are lost and it is then time to get down on your knees, and start praying. Sometimes it happens quickly, and people respond quickly – sometimes people are reluctant to humble themselves to God, and it might go on for days, weeks, months, or maybe even years, but God is persistent; no one will have to explain that to you, because you will *know*, and *understand* at that time that you are a sinner – lost, and in dyer need of a savior, and my advice to you is not to fight it, because it just causes unnecessary misery in your life, and God is under no obligation to continue offering people chances, so when he calls you need to answer by crying out to him – talking to him as if he were right in front of you – confessing the fact that you are a sinner – asking his forgiveness – dedicating yourself to repentance from your sins, and putting your trust in him to save you from an eternity in hell. When it gets to this point, you stay on your knees, and keep praying until salvation comes, and believe me, when it comes you'll know it; it will be as if the entire weight of this sinful world has been lifted off your shoulders, and there will be a peace in your heart that you've never felt before in your life! Just don't ignore God, because you don't know how much time you have here in this world, and you don't know if he will continue giving you chances."

"Is that the Holy Spirit that gives you that feeling?" She asked.

"Yes it is." I answered. "There are things in this life that can make us feel real good, but nothing compares to the sweet peace of the Holy Spirit, and this is how someone *knows* they're saved by the grace of God. Your life will be forever changed at the moment of salvation; 2 Corinthians 5:17 says, 'Therefore if any man be in Christ, he is a new creature: old things are passed away; behold, all things are become new.' You will see things in a different light from then on, because Jesus resides in your heart, and turning from your sins is made possible by this new influence, and desire to please God. This doesn't mean that you will automatically stop sinning, because you're still human, it's just that the Holy Spirit will now convict you of your sins – letting you know that whatever you're doing is unpleasing to God; Ezekiel 36:27 says, 'And I will put my spirit within you, and cause you to walk in my statutes, and ye shall keep my judgments, and do them.' The gift of Salvation is the greatest gift ever given to man, and it's because God loves us; John 3:16 says, 'For God so loved the world, that he gave his only begotten Son, that whosoever believeth in him should not perish, but have everlasting life.' And everlasting life is a good thing for those who believe. I look at this world around us, and think to myself how beautiful it is in its purity, but no one on the face of this earth can comprehend what awaits us after death; 1 Corinthians 2:9 says, 'But as it is written, Eye hath not seen, nor ear heard, neither have entered into the heart of man, the things which God hath prepared for them that love him.'"

Tim and Carmen both sat there in silence for a moment. I could tell that God's word was making its way into their hearts, and maybe even starting to make them aware of their need for Jesus Christ in their lives.

"Things are becoming very clear to me right now, and I know I have some soul searching to do." Carmen explained, "It seems like I've spent so much energy trying to prove the non-existence of the Christian God, that I've missed out on knowledge, which may have altered the course of my life."

"I kind of feel the same way." Tim added. "You have taught us more than I would have ever believed, and I really hope we haven't done harm to our friends and family by being a negative influence on them."

"Don't worry about that." I tried to console them. "What's in the past is in the past, and if you give your lives to Jesus he will change you, and all those that you have influence with will see that change, then who knows what great things God can do with their lives. It is a wonderful thing when someone who was previously an atheist or an agnostic gives their life to Jesus Christ, because there is a major change that takes place in their mannerisms, and basically their entire lifestyle that is impossible for their friends and family to ignore. Sometimes you may lose contact with friends or family members due to the fact that they choose to continue rejecting God, and therefore anyone who is promoting God's kingdom, but that is a choice they will be responsible for, and it is all the more reason to continue reaching out to them with love any chance you get. Christians are to be a light in this world, and we are not to hide this light from anyone – especially from those who do not know Jesus. Jesus says in Mathew 5:14, 16, 'Ye are the light of the world. A city that is set on a hill cannot be hid. Let your light so shine before men, that they may see your good works, and glorify your Father which is in heaven.' Those who are lost need to see the light that can only be given by Christians even if they say or do evil things against us, because in the end it will glorify God as it says in 1 Peter 2:12 which states, 'Having your conversation honest among the Gentiles: that, whereas they speak against you as evildoers, they may by your good works, which they shall behold, glorify God in the day of visitation.'"

Carmen looked at Tim with a humble look of expectance as she said, "Maybe we need to look for a church to start going to when we get home."

She waited – hoping he would feel the same way I'm sure. After a short pause he turned his gaze to me and said, "I think that would be a good idea, but since there are so many churches out there, how do we know which one to attend?" He asked.

"I'm glad to hear you two say that." I said smiling. "Finding a church is very important, because it helps us grow in the Lord, and being in fellowship with other believers helps

Christians maintain strength, and gives positive affirmation. Hebrews 10:25 says, 'Not forsaking the assembling of ourselves together, as the manner of some is; but exhorting one another: and so much the more, as ye see the day approaching.' This is telling Christians not to stop gathering together as some have, but we need to exhort one another, and we all need to hear the word of God preached, because it pleases God as it says in 1 Corinthians 1:21, 'For after that in the wisdom of God the world by wisdom knew not God, it pleased God by the foolishness of preaching to save them that believe.' Even though preaching is considered foolishness in God's eyes – it is necessary to please the Lord, and save souls. Now to answer your question about how to find the *right* church, I'm going to just give you some essentials to look for, which should help you, but it may take some searching to find what you would consider 'the right one'. I would say there are four definite essentials that a church must have; one would be a congregation with the desire to truly worship God, and not some place set up to entertain or promote mere socializing of its members. To worship God is to give him honor, and glorify *his* name – not our own; second would be a pastor who is dedicated to preaching God's word as it is written, and preaching what God gives him to preach, not taking things into his own hands, and leaving God out of it. He also needs to be someone who truly believes that the Holy Bible is *the inspired, infallible word of God* – you will know the Word of God, since you will now be reading your Bibles on a regular basis." I said as I looked into their eyes hoping for some affirmation of this.

They both smiled, and nodded their heads sending me the message that they really would try to dive into this new endeavor.

"The third essential for a good church would be a place that observes the sacraments – such as baptism and the Lords supper – and a place that practices church discipline, because without discipline, heresy will make its way into the church. Finally it needs to be a church that glorifies God in *songs* and more importantly *prayer.* When it comes to songs it will be up to your preference, because there are a lot of choices in that area; there are contemporary driven services, some sing the old time hymns, and there are some churches that incorporate both into their services, so you may need to experience all of it in order to make a choice, but beware of those churches that try to replace the Holy Spirit with feelings brought on by uplifting music. The last thing I mentioned was prayer, which cannot be emphasized enough; if a church does not beseech God in prayer for its leadership, and direction….it probably does not have much of a communion with God, and therefore is not going to be beneficial to its attendants."

"Since you mentioned prayer, I have a question about that." Tim said. "I don't really understand why prayer is necessary since God already knows everything that is going to happen – I mean what good is asking God for something if he already knows the outcome of any given situation?"

"That's a very good question Tim, and yes God does know everything that we are going to ask before we ask it; Mathew 6:8 says, 'Be not ye therefore like unto them: for your Father knoweth what things ye have need of, before ye ask him.' There are many scriptures that address prayer, and the fact that we are instructed to pray is enough of a reason, but I will try to paint you a picture that will illuminate the necessity of a healthy prayer life. When you think about your relationship with Carmen, what do you think would happen if you didn't talk to her, or maybe the only time you made an effort to talk to her was when you wanted something from her?"

Carmen had an eager look on her face awaiting Tim's response to this question, but there was also a smirk that that showed a playful intent.

"If I didn't speak to her at all I'm pretty certain that our relationship wouldn't last very long, and if I only spoke to her when I needed something I'm sure she would feel used, and again would result in a very short relationship." He answered, and Carmen nodded in agreement with his response.

"Good answer." She said smiling.

"I'd say that's a very reasonable assumption, because without constant communication a relationship is not possible." I said. "This also holds true for a person's relationship with God. We can't expect to have a relationship if we don't communicate, but think about this – if a person truly loves God they will *want* constant communication, and there should be a desire to pray, because if there's not….maybe a re-evaluation of priorities is necessary."

"That makes sense," He said. "I hadn't thought about it that way; I guess there are a lot of people who only pray when they're in trouble or wanting something, then they wonder why they don't get what they asked for – like you talked about a moment ago."

"Exactly." I agreed. "There is a circle of communication that includes praying, and meditating on the Word of God. We speak to God through prayer, and God speaks to us through his word, which reveals to us his will, and then we must pray in accordance with his will in order for our prayers to be answered. 1 John 5:14-15 states, 'And this is the confidence that we have in him, that, if we ask anything according to his will, he heareth us: And if we know that he hear us, whatsoever we ask, we know that we have the petitions that we desired of him.' Then Jesus says in Mathew 7:7-8, 'Ask, and it shall be given you; seek, and ye shall find; knock, and it shall be opened unto you: For everyone that asketh receiveth; and he that seeketh findeth; and to him that knocketh it shall be opened.' Even though God knows the beginning from the end, the Bible is very clear on the fact that prayer will have results as it says in James 5:16, 'Confess your faults one to another, and pray one for another, that ye may be healed. The effectual fervent prayer of a righteous man availeth much.'"

"I guess praying for a million dollars is out of the question." Tim stated with a hint of laughter.

"Well, praying for money might not be what God wants for you, however, if giving you money will lead to promoting God's kingdom, because of the way you appropriate it, then you just might get it; God knows your heart, and knows if you can handle riches, and whether or not you will be a good steward of it, so he'll have to decide on that one."

"I know we're getting short on time," Carmen said with regret. "But there's one thing that I don't believe has been mentioned, and that's baptism; is baptism the same as salvation – or a necessity of salvation?"

"Actually the answer to that is neither; a person who gets baptized, but has not been saved first, only gets wet. The Bible is very clear that we are saved by grace through faith, as we talked about earlier – no work we do, such as baptism, will save us, however, Jesus instructed us to be baptized in Mathew 28:19,20 which says, 'Go ye therefore, and teach all nations, baptizing them in the name of the Father, and of the Son, and of the Holy Ghost: Teaching them to observe all things whatsoever I have commanded you: and, lo I am with you always, even unto the end of the world. Amen.' The reason for baptism is its symbolism; it signifies that a person has given their life to Jesus – the old self has died – going into, and being buried in the water, and is raised up a new creature being cleansed by the blood of Jesus Christ as Romans 6:4-13 describes, 'Therefore we are buried with him by baptism into death: that like as Christ was raised up from the dead by the glory of the Father, even so we also should walk in newness of life. For if we have been planted together in the likeness of his death, we shall be also in the likeness of his resurrection: Knowing this, that our old man is crucified with him, that the body of sin might be destroyed, that henceforth we should not serve sin. For he that is dead is freed from sin. Now if we be dead with Christ, we believe that we shall also live with him: Knowing that Christ being raised from the dead dieth no more; death hath no more dominion over him. For in that he died, he died unto sin once: but in that he liveth, he liveth unto God. Likewise reckon ye also yourselves to be dead indeed unto sin, but alive unto God through Jesus Christ our Lord. Let not sin therefore reign in your mortal body, that ye should obey it in the lusts thereof. Neither yield ye your members as instruments of unrighteousness unto sin: but yield yourselves unto God, as those that are alive from the dead, and your members as instruments of righteousness unto God.' So it is a good thing to be baptized if only for the fact that Jesus said so, but being saved is the most important thing by all means."

Chapter 10
The parting of ways

I looked at my watch and realized that the dreaded moment of our departure had finally come, and we would now need to be on our way so they could pick up their jeep, and continue on their journey.

"Well kids, I hate to say it but it is 4:30, and we'd better get you to the dealership before they close." I said as I made it to my feet.

"I guess I'll run in and gather our things." Carmen explained sadly. Tim was also getting to his feet, and it appeared that he had to force himself to do so.

"I'll help you baby," He said with hesitation. "I guess we can't put it off any longer."

"I wish we could keep going on myself," I explained. "But at least we have covered quite a bit of ground during your stay, which hopefully will help you out some, and now you get to continue your original journey, and enjoy yourselves immensely in Gatlinburg."

They both smiled, and nodded as we entered the house. They retreated to their room for their belongings, and I collected my car keys from my nightstand.

The trip to the dealership was a lot quieter than any of our previous experiences – undoubtedly due to the sadness of the upcoming goodbyes.

"In case I haven't said so already….I'm very glad you kids broke down in front of my house." I stated in order to break the silence. "I'm sorry about the extra expenses you've incurred as a result of it, but glad it happened all the same."

"I'm glad it happened too," Tim said in a very positive manner, even though I could tell that he was trying to overcome the negative of the situation. "And I think the repair costs are going to be well worth it, since we may have never run into someone that could articulate things the way you have."

"I agree totally." Carmen said. "I guess God *does* work in mysterious ways, as the old saying goes. I'm sorry we've been quiet for the past few minutes….it's just that I'm going to miss our conversation….and the conversationalist of course." She said with a smile.

"I'm definitely going to miss you kids too, and if I can ever be of any assistance again, you know where to find me. I do think you at least have enough information now to be able to work things out for yourselves, and I hope I've conveyed the loving nature of our heavenly father in a way that will stick with you from now on."

"You've done a great job of that." Carmen said. "I think we now have a completely different view of Christianity than we had before thanks to you." She said while looking at Tim for re-enforcement, which he eagerly responded to with a smile, and nod.

Our facial expressions became somber once again as we pulled into the dealership adjacent to their jeep.

"I'll run inside, and take care of our bill, and then I'll come back and load up our luggage." Tim said as he stepped out of my car, and onto the curb.

"Don't worry about the luggage. "I said, getting out myself. "I'll start moving things into the jeep while you're inside."

Carmen and I shuffled the luggage back into its original abode while trying to keep our conversation cheerful in the midst of our sadness. After a few minutes, Tim reappeared – keys in hand, and the look of farewell on his face.

"We're all set baby." He said to Carmen, and then turned to me with an outstretched hand. "We've got a long ride ahead of us, so I guess we'd better get started."

I shook his hand gladly and said, "It's been a real pleasure, and I wish you kids a safe trip, and a very happy life."

"The pleasure was all ours." He responded, and then I turned to Carmen who was already reaching out for a hug. As we embraced I felt the cold wet sensation of a tear that was being transferred from her cheek to mine as she allowed her emotions to surface.

"It's ok." I told her – patting her on the back. "Even though it's goodbye for now, it's also a new beginning for each of us as we choose our path of tomorrow, and if we don't meet again in this life….I expect to see you both in the next."

"I know." She said, drying her tears with a napkin that Tim had given her. "I just don't like goodbyes."

"No one does," I explained. "However, you know where I live, and I'm going to give you my number, so you can contact me anytime – day or night."

I grabbed a pen, and a piece of paper from the car, and began writing my number on it; Tim also wrote their number on a business card, so we could keep in touch, and after exchanging numbers he helped Carmen into her seat.

"Thank you so much for taking care of us during our unplanned stay in Blue Ridge." He said as he made his way around to the driver's seat.

"Yes Jack, you have been wonderful to us, and I hope one day we can return the favor." Carmen said as Tim turned the key, and started the engine.

The rumbling exhaust brought back many memories of my past love for the off road.

"If you'll keep God's word close to your heart, and give him a chance to change you lives….consider the favor returned."

"Deal." She said as they began backing out of the parking space.

As they drove away we all exchanged a quick wave, and then they were gone. This had been such a wonderful experience for me, and now it was up to the Lord to water, and nurture the seed that had been planted.

On my way home I couldn't help but smile, even though I was sad to see them go, because I had chosen to do the will of God by witnessing to them, and there is always a blessing in store for those who do the will of the Lord. There's a feeling that comes with obedience, which is hard to describe, and it seems like the harder the task is – the more potent the blessing afterwards.

I also know from trial and error that witnessing experiences are not always pleasant, and it can be very discouraging when someone who has hardened their heart towards God says, or does something very rude or hateful to the person witnessing, but we must be diligent, because they are sinners, and that's what sinners sometimes do. Jesus said in John 9:4, "I must work the works of him that sent me, while it is day: the night cometh, when no man can work." So this should be a lesson to us all, because there is a day coming when God is going to put an end to things here on this earth, and then no one will be able to do the work for him they've been putting off. If there's a family member, or friend, or co-worker that has not been saved, and maybe we've been meaning to witness to them, but just haven't gotten around to it....it will be too late; they will no longer have a chance to make things right with God, and we will have missed out on an opportunity to pass along the wonderful gift of the gospel of Jesus Christ.

I have missed out on many experiences myself over the years, but I'm glad that I finally realized my place in the body of Christ, and now things that once scared me....no longer have control over me.

Sometimes I wonder how it seems that the world can grab hold of us so easily – luring us in with anything the human heart could want, and it always seems that there are plenty of people willing to pull us down into this destructive life with them.... telling us how wonderful it is, and how the Bible thumpers are missing out on all the fun, *knowing themselves* how close they are to the sorrow, and pain that generally follow temporary pleasures in this type of lifestyle. It can be so hard to make a stand for God being seemingly surrounded by these opposing forces trying to tear us down every chance they get, but we have to prove our allegiance to God, and many don't have the courage it takes to make that stand, so they continue blending in with the world. Jesus said in Mathew 7:13, "Enter ye in at the strait gate: for wide is the gate, and broad is the way, that leadeth to destruction, and many there be which go in thereat: Because strait is the gate, and narrow is the way, which leadeth unto life, and few there be that find it." And he says in Mathew 16:24, "Then said Jesus unto his disciples, If any man will come after me, let him deny himself, and take up his cross, and follow me." So in essence he's telling us that the strait and narrow way is the path less traveled – not followed by the crowd, and we will have to bear our own cross in order to follow him, but after the pain, suffering, and ridicule that Jesus suffered for us – who do not deserve his mercy in the least – we should be more than happy to put up with a little difficulty here on earth, in order to glorify him.

While driving back home I wondered what their conversation consisted of as they made their way through the mountains. I know the power of the Word of God, so I'm sure that it was working in their hearts and minds, but nonetheless, I still wished I could hear the conversation between them.

It's hard sometimes to work at something – putting your time, and passion into it, but not being there to reap the harvest; however, the body of Christ must work together for him, and sometimes it will be someone else who gets to see the end result – not the one who planted the seed. This is how God works, and he knows what he's doing, so we can be proud that we've done our part for him, no matter how small a part it is.

Chapter 11
The good news

The days continued to pass by, eventually turning to weeks – very uneventful I might add, but all in all I guess everything was back to normal. The festivals moved on, and the residents glided back into their everyday routines. I myself was back to spending a good part of my days sitting on the front porch in my favorite rocker – people watching, and catching up on the latest news in the local paper.

From time to time I would glance over to the swing and think of Tim and Carmen sitting there eagerly awaiting answers to all the questions brought on by our culture, and many other variables in their lives, wondering how they were getting along after our time spent together, and I remember thinking that it was about time for me to give them a call just to see how they were doing. There was a part of me that thought by doing this it would seem as though I were being nosy, and offend them in some way, but that's what Satan would love for me to think. It would make him happy for me to allow a thought like this to keep me from communicating with someone who just might need to hear something. In any case, we said we would keep in touch, so I wasn't about to allow the devil to work his magic.

I was so involved in my thoughts about this subject that a sudden noise from behind me caught me off guard, causing me to jump nearly out of my seat. It was the phone ringing inside the house. After regaining my composure, I started in the house, all the time wondering who it might be. I don't get a lot of phone calls, since I prefer most of my encounters with friends and family to be face to face, so there is always a mixture of feelings when I hear that ring; part of me is exited to hear a familiar voice, and there is always a slight dread in the back of my mind – wondering if there will be bad news coming from the other end of the line.

I haven't caught up with technology yet, so caller ID is not an available option on my antiquated jewel of a phone, but that doesn't bother me since I always enjoy a rather excited feeling of not knowing who is on the other end. When I picked up the hand set it was such a joy when I heard Carmen's voice on the other end.

"Hi Jack, it's Carmen." She said, with sheer excitement in her voice.

"Well, hello Carmen." I responded cheerfully. "It's great to hear from you; I was just thinking about you two, and I had just made up my mind to call you myself."

"Well, we all know how God works in mysterious ways." She said laughing. There was also something else projecting from her voice; I could feel that there was a purpose for this phone call well beyond the promise to keep in touch, and this purpose had not yet been revealed; it was creating a sense of growing anticipation on my end. "We've been meaning to call before now, but we sort of let our busy lives get the best of us."

"That's ok." I said. "I've been meaning to do the same, but talked myself out of it – not wanting to bother you."

"You couldn't bother us if you tried," She explained. "After taking care of us the way you did."

There was a short pause, as she almost seemed to be working up the courage for something, and then all at once, as if the pressure had reached its maximum, the words started flowing almost uncontrollably.

"I just had to call you, and let you know the news....it's wonderful....I can't explain it....I'm sorry for rambling, but I'm just so overwhelmed...."

"Ok, just slow down a little, and tell me what's going on." I said slowly, in hopes of helping her calm down, and better articulate her words.

"I GOT SAVED LAST NIGHT!" She said almost screaming in my ear.

"Are you serious? That's wonderful. You have no idea how happy it makes me to hear that." I said, overflowing with joy. "Tell me all about it."

I so eagerly waited to hear all the details. It is such a wonderful thing when Jesus brings one of his lost sheep into the fold.

"Well, Tim and I have been visiting a different church every week since we got home from Gatlinburg, and we've even been occasionally going on Wednesday nights, hoping to find the right one; a couple of weeks ago we visited a church – not too far from home – that we both felt very comfortable in, and it seemed to be more like a large family that was eager to welcome us back home after an extended absence or something, rather than looking at us as outsiders, and we've both noticed a profuse amount of similarities between the pastors sermons, and our conversations on your front porch. I had really enjoyed listening to him preach on Sunday mornings, but last night was different; it's hard to explain, but I could tell something wasn't normal before we even left home. I told Tim that maybe I was coming down with something, even though it really didn't feel the same as a prelude to sickness, and then as we took our seats and the singing began I was seemingly overwhelmed with a sense of worry. I think this is the point where I began thinking about death, and it was so clear to me that no matter how good I'd been in the past....if I died right then I was going to hell, which made me feel very panicky, and I couldn't concentrate on the singing, or anything else going on around me for that matter; I just sat there with my stomach turning, hoping it would go away. The singing was starting to come to a close when I finally remembered what you had told me about how there would be no doubt in my mind when the Lord was drawing me, and I realized that I was fighting it by trying to make the uncomfortable feelings go away, but I was a little confused as to why this was happening now as opposed to later; I thought this kind of thing would happen after the preacher was done preaching, so I just sat there hoping I could hold off until then. When the pastor started making his way to the pulpit he suddenly stopped – turned around to face the congregation – then laid his Bible back on the pew, and picked up a hymnal. He was silent for a moment, which seemed like an eternity to me – considering the shape I was in – then as he turned the pages in the hymnal he said, 'I know you are expecting me to get up there and preach, and who knows, maybe I will in a moment, but right now I'm feeling a strong presence of the Holy Spirit leading me to sing another song, so I think the best thing for me to do is be obedient. Let's all stand, and sing a couple verses of Amazing Grace, then we'll see where it goes from there.'

When I stood up my knees were so weak, and shaking like a leaf, so when the singing started I couldn't take it any more; I almost ran to the altar….crying, and just like you said, it felt as though my heart was being pulled out of my chest. The pastor knelt down with me as the singing continued, and I think there were a few others that joined us, but my only thoughts were to beg Jesus for forgiveness, and mercy, and I wanted to commit my life to him from then on. I don't know how long we were down there, but all the sudden there was a peace that came over me….I don't even know how to begin to explain it, but I felt that there was no need to worry anymore, and felt a happiness that I *never ever* remember feeling at any other time in my life….I actually felt like I could fly at that moment, but instead I was busy being hugged by the pastor, and blown away by the joy that the whole church seemed to be feeling at that moment. I had always thought it would be embarrassing to be in front of a church full of people, talking about some personal matter, but when the pastor asked me to tell the congregation what I'd experienced, it was surprisingly easy, and was a relief to get off my chest."

"That's wonderful, because confessing your salvation is very important; Jesus said in Mathew 10:32, 33, 'Whosoever therefore shall confess me before men, him will I confess also before my Father which is in heaven. But whosoever shall deny me before men, him will I also deny before my Father which is in heaven.' Another good one is Romans 10:9, 10 which says, 'That if thou shalt confess with thy mouth the Lord Jesus, and shalt believe in thine heart that God hath raised him from the dead, thou shalt be saved. For with the heart man believeth unto righteousness; and with the mouth confession is made unto salvation.'"

I was so happy for her at that moment. I know salvation is between an individual, and God….and we should never assume that we know if someone is saved or not, but everything inside me was telling me that this was genuine, and I was so glad to have been a part of her experience. I can remember when Jesus changed my life, and how good it felt inside, so hearing Carmen describe that very same feeling is just another re-enforcement to the beliefs of Christianity.

"I am so happy for you Carmen, and it will be a wonderful experience for you to begin developing your relationship with God; meditate on his word every day and let him speak to you, and guide you in your walk of life, because he knows what's best for you even if you don't. I'm reminded of Isaiah 30:21 which says, 'And thine ears shall hear a word behind thee, saying, This is the way, walk ye in it, when ye turn to the right hand, and when ye turn to the left.' And then Psalms 48:14 says, 'For this God is our God for ever and ever: he will be our guide even unto death.'"

"I just hope I won't mess things up, and do the wrong things." She said.

"Well, I'll go ahead and tell you that you *will* mess things up sometimes, because your human like the rest of us, but don't let Satan use that against you; when he reminds you of how imperfect you are....think about what his future entails, and that will make you feel better."

"So, what will God's direction sound like? Am I going to hear voices, or is it going to feel like what I felt last night?" She asked.

"That is totally up to God's discretion." I answered. "As you read the scriptures, you'll notice that God has used many different ways to communicate with his people over time; he carried on conversations with some, a small still voice with others, and sometimes he may use an earthquake to get someone's attention. As I told you before, the Bible is God's word, and I would say the most used method of communication with us, even though he is capable of using whatever method he desires. If you will continue to meditate on his word, and pray to him, he will reveal things to you as needed. Anyone who has been a Christian for any length of time can vouch for me on this one....you may have read a certain scripture a thousand times in the past, and nothing came of it, but all of the sudden one day you're dealing with some situation – praying for answers, or help, and then there it is....the answer is revealed to you in a passage that never registered with you before. God does things in his own way, and on his time schedule – not ours – so just stay close to him, and he won't have to use an earthquake to talk to you."

"I guess I just have to trust him, since he knows what he's doing, and I don't. I'm sure you've had some great experiences with God over the years, Jack."

"I definitely have, and each time I seem to learn a little more about his ways; for example, I was always a very impatient young man in my early days, and I knew this was not a thing to be proud of, so one day as I was praying, I asked the Lord to please help me develop my patience; now I assumed that if God decided to answer this prayer, he would just magically embed patience into my personality or something, but I was very wrong about that."

"What happened?" She asked.

"Well, that turned out to be the worst day I'd had in a long time. Everything seemingly went wrong. I had people yelling at me, everything I touched seemed to break down on me, and I just couldn't get anything accomplished. I lost my temper many times throughout these events, and in my mind I questioned God over and over without response. Finally I made it home that evening, and decided that I would just sit on the couch, watch T.V., and try to forget about my troubles, but I was wrong about that too. Questioning God's judgment was wrong, and that disobedience was sinful, so the Holy Spirit was convicting me of that, and I began to feel remorse for my behavior. I had to make things right with God, so I got down on my knees, and began to ask his forgiveness, and also asking him to help me deal with this apparent fault in my life. His reply to me couldn't have come any clearer; there were two scriptures that came into my mind – James 1:2-4, and Romans 5:3,4 which say, 'My brethren, count it all joy when ye fall into divers temptations; Knowing this, that the trying of your faith worketh patience. But let patience have her perfect work, that ye may be perfect and entire, wanting nothing. And not only so, but we glory in tribulation also: knowing that tribulation worketh patience; And patience, experience: and experience, hope:'"

"You actually got exactly what you asked for, and didn't even know it." She said, and I was very proud that she picked up on that.

"Yes I did." I replied. "I just had to get down on my knees in order to realize it. God does work in mysterious ways, and we have to be ready for whatever that is. Instead of just giving me the patience I had asked for, he gave me situations that would allow my patience to develop, but I had to get out of my own way in order to understand that. Many times we are blinded by our anger, self-pity, or worry to the point that we miss the lesson God is giving us. If you ask for courage….he just might give you a scary situation that will allow your undiscovered courage to show itself, so be looking, and asking for the revelation of his will so that you won't miss the purpose of the tribulations he allows in your life."

"I guess we wouldn't appreciate it as much if he just gave us what we wanted without any work on our part." She added.

"That's right. The Lord helps those who help themselves, which means there will be some effort required from us. While we remain on this earth, we are in training, and God is helping us develop our character, and molding us into what he wants us to be, so it is important that we don't fight him on this; always pray that his will is done in your life – not yours, and also pray that he will reveal to you what he wants you to do with your life – not what you want to do with it."

" I was also thinking back to something you said on your porch about knowledge; I guess now that my knowledge is starting to increase, there will also be more expected of me, correct?"

"That's right." I answered. "But that's not a negative, as some would lead you to believe. If you want to experience the fullness of a relationship with God, you must grow in the knowledge of his ways, and since you are now a child of God, he will guide you as a father should, which means there will be lessons to learn, and correction if you start wandering in the wrong direction. If you just sit back in the safe zone, not trying to grow as a Christian, you will not experience the life God has planned for you, which will be exactly what Satan wants you to do now that he can't have you, however, there's no limit to what God can give you if you truly humble yourself, and allow him to be the direction in your life from now on."

"Right now humbling myself and pleasing God is all I want to do. I hope that doesn't change." She said.

"Stay close to God, and he'll keep you close to him. When you start working for God, and things seem to be going well, just remember what you just said, because it's very easy to exalt yourself – taking the credit for the work God is doing in your life.

Mathew 23:12 says, 'And whosoever shall exalt himself shall be abased; and he that shall humble himself shall be exalted.'"

"I really can't wait to tell all my friends what has happened, and teach them some of the things I've learned, so that maybe they'll want to change their lives too." She said, with obvious excitement in her voice.

"That kind of attitude and drive is very important, but I want you to be prepared for things that might happen. There are many people out there, including family and friends, that have hardened their hearts toward God, or in some cases God has chosen to harden their hearts, and they will be unwilling to accept anything that will expect them to give up their love affair with the sins in their lives. Jesus even felt grief for the Pharisees, because of the hardness of their hearts, which caused them not to see the true purpose of his teachings, and miracles. I myself lost some friends, and was mocked in my youth, because I was trying to spread the gospel of Jesus Christ, and this caused me to lose a lot of that drive that is so necessary in doing God's work. It took me many years to get back where I should be, so I don't want you to let these types of disappointments have the same effect on you. If you go into this knowing that rejection is a real possibility, then you can overcome it by your dedication to God. If you keep a strong attitude towards working for God, you will be fruitful; In John 15:5 Jesus says, 'I am the vine, ye are the branches: He that abideth in me, and I in him, the same bringeth forth much fruit: for without me ye can do nothing.'"

"The preacher did say that by accepting Jesus, I would be able to harness some of his strength to fight against adversity, and putting my faith in him was like building my house upon the rock."

"That's right. Jesus said in Mathew 7:24, 25, 'Therefore whosoever heareth these sayings of mine, and doeth them, I will liken him unto a wise man, which built his house upon a rock: And the rain descended, and the floods came, and the winds blew, and beat upon that house; and it fell not: for it was founded upon a rock.' The criticism, and negativity that God's children sometimes experience can be compared to the rains, winds, and floods described by Jesus, but since he is now your anchor, you will be able to withstand these forces."

"I guess I just don't need to take things too personal when witnessing to others." She said in a questioning manner.

"Well, that's kind of hard to do." I said, searching for the proper response to her statement. "Because it is personal to all of us who are saved. What I mean is this, once a person has given their life to God they cannot help but feel love for all God's creations – especially human beings – and because we feel this love, we feel the necessity to lead them to Christ so that they will experience eternal life with him; we don't want to see them throw their life away, and end up with Hell as their final destination. If we didn't care, then we wouldn't bother taking the chance of being rejected, but we also have to realize that we are only responsible for *spreading* the gospel of Jesus Christ to those who are lost….we are not responsible for the choices that those people make in response."

"I guess there's a fine line that we have to be aware of." She added. "We can be content knowing that we have done what God wants us to do, and if we are rejected, because of someone else's free will, we can feel bad for them, but we shouldn't let that stop us from continuing on."

"That's as good of an outlook as any I've heard." I commended her. "Once we've done our part they are in God's hands, and who knows, we may be expected to witness to them more in the future, or God may send someone else their way to continue the process. You won't always see the fruit of your labors, but we are not commissioned to do all the harvesting….just to spread the good news about Jesus."

Chapter 12
What about Tim?

After a moments pause I realized that I was so overcome with the excitement of Carmen's good news that I had totally neglected to inquire about Tim; after all we were in this together, and I was curious as to whether or not he had experienced anything.

"You know Carmen, it has totally slipped my mind to ask about Tim." I said apologetically. "How's he doing during all of this?"

"Well, that's something else I wanted to talk to you about. He's told me how happy he is for me, and I know that he is sincere, but I can tell he's holding back something. I think he's a little concerned that it hasn't happened to him."

"Why do you say that?" I asked.

"We were talking to the preacher after service about scheduling my baptism, and he asked Tim if he would *also* be interested in joining the church; I think he was assuming that Tim was also saved, but when Tim told him that he wasn't, I could tell that the meaning of that really hit home. Later on after we left church, he said that maybe he had waited too long, and God had given up on him or something; I think maybe he figured it would happen to both of us at the same time."

"Sounds like he's thinking God behaves in the same way that a man would – using the same type of organizational mannerisms. Is he there so I can talk to him, and maybe help him out a little?" I asked.

"No." She replied. "He's over at a friend's house helping cut some trees down or something."

"Well, I guess you can relay some thoughts to him later, and maybe it will help him. This is all new to both of you, and you will have to realize that God is not on any type of time schedule, so things might not take place the way or time you think they should. The fact that it is bothering him is a good thing, and God will draw him when he is ready to, because it is promised in God's Word. Deuteronomy 4:29 is one of many verses that describe this promise. Moses tells the children of Israel, 'But if from thence thou shalt seek the Lord thy God, thou shalt find him, if thou seek him with all thy heart and with all thy soul.' God wants us to seek him, and there is a celebration in heaven when someone repents, and turns to Jesus. Jesus said in Luke 15:7, 'I say unto you, that likewise joy shall be in heaven over one sinner that repenteth, more than over ninety nine just persons, which need no repentance.' I believe I told you kids when you were here that God searches the heart, and he knows what is really going on inside of us whether we admit it or not; the fact that Tim is concerned about this means he may be seeking God, and is probably in the beginning stages of God's drawing power, however, he may not have the same exact experience that you or anyone else has, because God knows what kind of experience Tim needs in order for his will to be done. I think *you* were seeking God a long time ago, but maybe didn't realize it; Tim may just be getting to that point, and we have to trust God to take care of him. In 1 Chronicles 28:9 King David was speaking to his son Solomon about seeking God, and the matters of the heart and mind; it says, 'And thou, Solomon my son, know thou the God of thy father, and serve him with a perfect heart and with a willing mind: for the Lord searcheth all hearts, and understandeth all the imaginations of the thoughts: if thou seek him, he will be found of thee; but if thou forsake him, he will cast thee off for ever.' So let him know that he needs to keep on seeking, and he will find the Lord when it is time."

"I'll definitely tell him that." She said. "I just hope he gets to experience this soon, so that we can start growing as Christians *together* instead of the alternative."

"I'm sure things will work out just the way God wants them to. By the way, did you set a date for your baptism?" I asked.

"Yes we did actually; it's going to be three weeks from this Sunday right after church services. I really would love it if you could find a way to make it down here, since you're probably the reason it's happening in the first place."

"God is actually the reason it's happening; I just tried to do what I was led to do, and if I had failed I'm sure God would have found someone else who *was* willing, but everything else aside, I wouldn't miss it for the world. If you can give me some directions I'll put it on my calendar right now."

She gave me directions, and the name of the church, and I wrote them on the calendar in bright red letters, since this was such an important occasion.

"When Tim gets home tell him I said hello, and if you need anything between now and then just give me a call – I'd be glad to help out in any way I can."

"Thank you so much Jack, you have no idea how much it means to me to know you're going to be there. If you need anything the phone line runs both ways, so feel free to call us too."

"I will."

We hung up the phone, and I went back out onto the porch to continue my afternoon of leisure – still feeling a sense of excitement, because of the news I'd just heard. It had me feeling so good, and energetic that I decided maybe I would go for a walk around town – say hello to a few people, and collect my thoughts.

As I walked I thought about Jesus' Sermon on the Mount in Mathew chapter 5, which describes the attitude, and character that is an absolute description of true Christians, and I believe that Carmen is going to fit in just fine. I believe its verse 6, which says, "Blessed are they which do hunger and thirst after righteousness: for they shall be filled." And I can see her as being someone who will have a definite hunger, and thirst for the bread and water that only God can provide. Tim, on the other hand seems to be a little more guarded, which may be why the Lord is taking more time with him. Jesus said in Mark 10:14, 15, "But when Jesus saw it, he was much displeased, and said unto them, Suffer the little children to come unto me, and forbid them not: for of such is the kingdom of God. Verily I say unto you, Whosoever shall not receive the kingdom of God as a little child, he shall not enter therein." Some take this out of context and say that if you don't get saved when you're a child, you can't get saved, but what this actually refers to is the mindset a person has to have – child or adult – in order to accept Jesus, and a new way of life. Jesus used children as an example, because they tend to be more open minded to accept new things, and eager to learn new ways; as a person gets older we sometimes lose that open thought process, and close our minds to God. I don't want you to think I'm saying Tim is completely closed off, because I'm not; I just think he has more of a tendency to fight it, which may mean it will take more time for him to humble himself to God. The Israelites had to be humbled, and were reminded of that in Deuteronomy 8:2, which says, "And thou shalt remember all the way which the Lord thy God led thee these forty years in the wilderness, to humble thee, and to prove thee, to know what was in thine heart, whether thou wouldest keep his commandments, or no."

I really did hope that Tim would get things worked out with the Lord....sooner than forty years, because in reality his life depends on it – his eternal life that is – and it would also make things a lot easier for both of them if they are heading in the same direction. The apostle Paul says in 2 Corinthians 6:14, "Be ye not unequally yoked together with unbelievers: for what fellowship hath righteousness with unrighteousness? And what communion hath light with darkness?" I believe he says this because of the inevitable hardships that accompany relationships that do not share a common goal. A Christian that is married to a non-believer will have to be extremely strong in order to keep from being dragged down the path that carries them further from God instead of closer to him.

In a way it's kind of a good thing that it didn't happen to both of them at the same time, because this means that Tim wasn't willing to fake God's draw just because it may be more comfortable to go to the altar with his companion. Sometimes this sort of thing happens – especially with children; they want to be doing the same thing that their friend or sibling is doing, and not because of a legitimate draw from God. When this happens to a child, or adult, it can result in what's known as a false convert, which is bad for everyone. If someone is not truly converted, they will not be spiritually born again with the changes of heart and mind that make us children of God; they will generally not stay in the faith very long before they succumb to worldly desires, and end up being a negative voice for Christianity instead of a positive example. Many of us know someone who at one time professed salvation then turned away from it saying it didn't do anything for them, or maybe they couldn't tell any difference in their life. The reason it didn't do anything for them is because they were never saved in the first place. A lot of false converts tend to "lose their religion" after spending some time in our colleges, because there is such a prominent anti-God mindset among the professors and students; those students and professors who do hold true to their faith in God seem to be few and far between. Most tend to push the idea that the truth, along with God, are whatever each individual wants them to be, and unknowing to most of them, they are breaking one of the Ten Commandments, because they are in essence creating a false God; they're creating one that is more to their personal liking. We are all surrounded by the call of worldly pleasures, but a true Christian will not be fulfilled by the things of this world, even if they try to dabble in it, and the world will not like them either; 1 John 3:13 says, "Marvel not, my brethren, if the world hate you." This is very true, because the world is against God, and vice versa, so if God is in your heart you cannot love the world.

Too many churches have tried to blur the line between the world, and God by turning places of worship into entertainment centers, hoping that the lost will be drawn in, but in many cases they have only managed to take God out their church by doing things their way instead of his, and at the same time they've taken away the distinguishing characteristics that should make Christians stand out against a background of the world. If you can't tell the difference between a sinner and a saint, why would you think Christianity is a better way of life? The church is there to worship God, and to feed believers with the Word of God – preparing them to go out into the streets and evangelize to those who need to hear the truth. When we do our jobs correctly on the streets, God will lead them into the churches where they can hopefully hear the gospel preached by someone called of God to do just that.
1 John 2:16, 17 says, "For all that is in the world, the lust of the flesh, and the lust of the eyes, and the pride of life, is not of the Father, but is of the world. And the world passeth away, and the lust thereof: but he that doeth the will of God abideth for ever." So let's not blend in too much with the world, because it will pass away.

I think everyone should read the book of 1 John, because it is not only a means to bring strength to believers, but it also helps bring to light any deviant forms of Christianity.

It talks about how God is light and has no darkness, so if someone claims to be of God but constantly walks in darkness, they are lying. Those who are saved still sin, but if they are walking in the light with God, the Holy Spirit will convict their heart of these sins and steer them towards repentance. I saw a bumper sticker once that read "Christians are not perfect – just forgiven." 1 John also talks about those who claim they do not sin, and it says the truth is not in them. It is a good book to read if you would like to take a test concerning your faith.

I guess I got a little side tracked there, but all in all I was fairly certain that Tim was smart enough to do the right things, and hopefully apply some of the wisdom that was quoted to him from God's Word while they were here, and I'm sure Carmen is very anxious for all this to take place.

I knew Carmen was also excited about witnessing to her friends, family, and anyone else she comes across – she should be – but sometimes that's not an easy road, even though it is a necessary one. I wasn't sure what kind of lifestyle the Conley's led up until our meeting, but it's possible that their friends will not be willing to listen to her new views, nor will they want to hang around them if they can't party like old times, but that's ok....as long as she stands firm on the principles of the Lord Jesus Christ, he'll help her through it.

When someone gets saved it doesn't mean that all life's problems are over, and everything will be a bed of roses from then on, sometimes it's just the opposite. We still have to deal with the same troubles and trials that everyone is exposed to, but we can call on Jesus for help, and comfort. We sometimes lose people that we care about, because our refusal to live in sin with them makes us "no fun anymore" and they don't want us to talk about God around them, because it makes them feel uncomfortable.

At times people can be downright harsh to us, because of our beliefs, but that's ok it's happened to many great people before us, and it will continue until Satan is cast into the lake of fire. We need to spread the word no matter what the consequence, because we are the salt of the earth, and the light to the lost; Jesus said in Mathew 5:11-14, "Blessed are ye, when men shall revile you, and persecute you, and shall say all manner of evil against you falsely, for my sake. Rejoice, and be exceeding glad: for great is your reward in heaven: for so persecuted they the prophets which were before you. Ye are the salt of the earth: but if the salt have lost his savor, wherewith shall it be salted? It is thenceforth good for nothing, but to be cast out, and to be trodden under foot of men. Ye are the light of the world. A city that is set on a hill cannot be hid."

I don't want to sound discouraging either....that's definitely not my intention, but I believe in telling it like it is so that surprises are kept to a minimum. Rejection is a part of life, and we can never know for sure how someone will react to a witness experience until the moment presents itself. Many times it turns into a very positive experience, even if only the seed was planted in his or her mind. We must be diligent, because it may take days, or weeks, or even years for that seed to germinate – causing the person to start searching for the truth....ultimately leading them to God, and if it happens to be a friend or family member that previously walked out of your life, you just might find them at your door step thanking you for sharing the gospel with them.

I guess what I'm saying is trust in the Lord no matter what. If you feel that the Lord is leading you to witness to someone....do it....no questions asked....even if you're afraid they will not respond in a way that is comfortable to you, because only God knows the outcome. Proverbs 3:5, 6 says, "Trust in the Lord with all thine heart; and lean not unto thine own understanding. In all thy ways acknowledge him, and he shall direct thy paths."

Chapter 13
Carmen's baptism

The next three weeks seemed to just creep by like time always seems to do when you're looking forward to something. I decided that I didn't want to take any chances on being late or missing any part of Carmen's special day, so I drove on down to Mableton the night before. As soon as I was about fifty miles south of home I remembered why I live in the country. The traffic just became more, and more insane the closer I got to Atlanta, and I felt my blood pressure rising at a pace consistent with the rise in volume of cars.

After checking into the hotel, it took a good hour to relax and wind down from the agonizing ride, but I eventually did relax and began thinking about the next day.

I was looking forward not only to the baptism, but also to hear the pastor, who Carmen seemed very fond of. I hoped that they had found a good one who drew his strength from the Lord, and promoted the type of church they could grow in….supporting them as they ventured into their new life with God.

As Sunday morning came around, I grew more and more excited by the minute, and it brought back memories of the day of my own baptism. I had that jittery mix of excitement, and nervousness, which makes you want to just cut right to the chase immediately instead of driving yourself crazy waiting. I'm sure Carmen was feeling much the same way.

I checked out of the hotel early so I could be at the church when Tim and Carmen arrived, and it worked out well since I was there a half an hour before anyone arrived…just the way I like it.

I waited in my car until I heard the moan of that beautiful jeep that had inadvertently led the Conley's to me, and the excitement heated up again. It was so good to see them again, and as I stepped out of my Car, I was greeted with an intense hug from Carmen, who had obviously ran across the parking lot in order to get here so quick.

"Hey Jack, I'm so glad you made it." She said, all the while squeezing the breath out of me.

"The pleasure is all mine." I responded. "I wouldn't have missed this for the world."

"Baby, you've got to let him go so he can catch his breath." Tim said laughing at her.

"I'm sorry." She said as she loosened her grip on me. "I've always been a hugger."

"That's quite alright." I replied. "I'll take all the hugs you can give me. It's good to see you too Tim. How have you been?"

"I'm doing good. Thanks for asking."

As he said that I remembered Carmen telling me that she felt he was holding something back, and now I could see why. It was very subtle, but never the less the look on his face and tone of his voice alluded that there was something obviously on his mind.

"How have you been?" He asked.

"Wonderful." I answered. "Especially since I heard Carmen's news. I think I've been more excited than she has for this day to arrive."

"I don't know about that." She intervened.

"Well let's just say that I've been *almost* as excited as you."

"Ok, I'll accept that." She grinned.

"I'm very excited for her too; even though I may have not shown it as well as I ought to." Tim added, as he rubbed her on the shoulders, and gave an apologetic look.

"Is there any particular reason for not showing it?" I asked.

"Well, it's just that I'm somewhat concerned about whether or not I'll ever get saved. Carmen told me everything you explained to her on the phone a few weeks ago, and it makes sense, but I guess I'm just impatient....mixed with worried. To be honest with you, I don't know what to think."

"Tim, just like I told Carmen, the fact that you're concerned is a good thing; it means that the Lord is dealing with you already, and maybe he's trying to help you with your patience by making you face it head on. There is a three step process to being saved; a person must realize that they are lost, and in need of a savior – they must truly believe in their heart that Jesus Christ came here as God in the flesh in order to be that savior by his death and resurrection, and then they must repent from their sins with the help of the Lord by trusting, and allowing him to work within them. It's obvious that you have reached step one, because you now realize your need of a savior, and the Lord is showing you that you need to be worried, otherwise you wouldn't care. It's now up to *you* to trust him to take care of you – pray without ceasing – humble yourself to him, and when you reach that place in your heart where God wants you to be he'll save you. Sometimes it's hard for us as human beings to humble ourselves, because pride gets in the way. You need to make sure that you take that pride out of the equation….only then will you open your hearts door for Jesus to change your life."

"I think that's exactly what's happening." He said. "I believe I'm standing in my own way, but I don't know how to move out of the way."

"That's where prayer comes in Tim. I cannot emphasize prayer enough, because this is how you will overcome many obstacles that will distance you from the Lord. All these feelings that you're keeping bottled up inside need to be poured out to God, and this will begin the humbling process. Grown men by nature want to be problem solvers, and bare life's burdens independently without help from anyone, but we have to realize that salvation is something way too enormous for us to handle, and ultimately impossible for us to obtain through any work of our own. Not accepting this fact leads to far worse repercussions than there would be for refusing to stop, and ask for directions on a trip. We have to get it through our thick skulls that we are not in control – never have been, and never will be. Keep praying – asking Jesus to take this pride out of you're life, and if you really mean it, he'll do it. I find myself having to stop many times during the day, and pray for help or guidance with many different things, but it took me a long time to realize that I couldn't handle these things on my own. Now I don't give it a moments thought when it comes to trusting the Lord with any of life's problems that confront me. You will have to come to that same understanding, and when something is on your mind start praying, so that God can help you. It doesn't have to be a public thing, in fact it shows God how pure your prayers are when it's just you and him, but that doesn't mean to put off God's draw until you're in a more private setting by no means. If you feel that draw then don't hesitate….get down on your knees right then, and take care of things."

"I just wish I had the same confidence you do." Tim said, still with a distraught look on his face.

"You do have the necessary confidence;" I replied. "You just haven't discovered it yet. The best thing I can tell you right now is *just don't fight it* –pray, and let God handle it....he knows what he's doing."

Our attention was then drawn to a gold suburban pulling into the parking space adjacent to mine. Carmen obviously was happy to see this person, since a very noticeable smile developed across her face.

A young man probably in his late thirties stepped out of the vehicle, holding his Bible, and dressed immaculately. He too was sporting a very noticeable smile as he looked toward us.

"Jack, this is James. He's the pastor here, and the one who will be performing the baptism." Carmen said excitedly.

"Hello James, it's a pleasure to meet you." I said, as I reached out to shake his hand. "You apparently have made quite the impression on these two young folks."

"I don't know about that." He said smiling. "I think I've come in second compared to your influence; from what they tell me, you're the reason they've searched us out, and we are so happy to have them."

"I just tried to follow God's lead while they were with me, and then he must have steered them to you."

"Well, Carmen." James said, as he reached out to shake their hands. "Are you ready, and excited?"

"I'm ready, excited, and nervous all rolled into one." She answered.

"Nothing to be nervous about." He smiled. "Everything will be just the way God wants it, and all you have to do is follow my lead. Why don't you go ahead and put your spare clothes in the young adults Sunday school room, since that's where you'll be changing later."

"Ok." She said. "Are you going to sit with us Jack?"

"Of course I will. I'll be there in just a few minutes."

She and Tim made there way to the entrance of the church, and I turned back to James.

"I'm so happy those two have found a good church." I said.

"I'm very glad they found us also; they're good kids, and I just hope not to fail them. I can tell that Tim is having a hard time right now, and I'm hoping that he won't be far behind her."

"Yes, we were just talking about that before you drove up." I said. "I feel pretty confident that God is drawing him right now, but I think he's fighting it."

"I believe you're right. I've noticed during the alter call of the past couple services, that he's holding on to the pew in front of him so tight that his knuckles are turning white. I've tried to talk to him a little, and my conclusion is that he is afraid he'll go to the altar, and fail in some way. It's something I've found to be typical of adults who haven't been saved; they tend to over complicate the whole process, instead of leaving it up to God."

"It's a shame that our over analyzing minds can hinder us in such simple matters."

"Very true." He said smiling. "If people only knew the relief that was awaiting them they would feel silly about putting it off so long. I guess we better go on in, and get things started. If you need anything just let me know."

"I will, thanks."

We went inside, and I made my way down to the front where the Conley's were already sitting. I do have to say that there was a comfortable feeling about this church, and I could see why the Conley's felt at home – much better than a cold building lacking the guidance of the Holy Spirit. If you've ever walked into a church where man has taken over, and decided he can do things better than God, you know what I mean when I say it has a very cold feel to it. Even when they try to produce their own version of the feeling you get from the Holy Spirit by using inspirational music, and spirit coaches, it's still cold.

"I see you found us." Carmen said.

"I did. I just needed to talk with James for a moment, and find out whether or not you two have been behaving yourselves."

We all shared a quiet laugh at that statement.

As the singing started, then lead to a wonderful sermon, any reservations I may have been secretly harboring about the Conley's ability to choose a good Bible preaching church were laid to rest. James was definitely called by God to preach the gospel, and I enjoyed the witness of the Holy Spirit during the entire message. Every so often I would glance over at the Conley's, and it was always the same….Carmen would be focused intently on the sermon, and Tim looked as if he would soon collapse with anxiety. I so wished that I could do it for him, but that's not the way things work, however, there was something I could do; I felt a real need to go to the altar myself, and pray for him to realize God's omnipotence in all things.

As soon as the sermon was over, James asked for the choir to come up and sing an invitational, and what an invitational it was. They started singing amazing grace, and my heart just lit up. I love all kinds of music, but that song holds a special place in my heart, because God's grace *is* amazing, and none of us deserve it, but he gives it to us freely. I believe it's Titus 3:5-7 that says, "Not by works of righteousness which we have done, but according to his mercy he saved us, by the washing of regeneration, and renewing of the Holy Ghost; Which he shed on us abundantly through Jesus Christ our Savior; That being justified by his grace, we should be made heirs according to the hope of eternal life." I not only wanted to pray for Tim, but I also wanted to thank the Lord for saving a wretch like me.

With tears in my eyes because of my overwhelming love for Jesus, I stepped out, and made my way to the altar. Apparently I wasn't the only one who needed this altar time, because several people from the congregation joined me. It was a sweet feeling as all those prayers started making their way to heaven, and I totally immersed myself in my own praise, and worship of my Lord. We prayed for some time, and all the sounds going on around me were somewhat of a blur – so much of a blur that I didn't realize who had knelt down beside me until I began to get up. I realized that Tim was at the altar with Carmen on one side, and James on the other – both with their arms across his shoulders – rubbing his back, and praying. I decided to stay down there with them to give my prayers and support – hopefully yielding a good outcome.

God promised to draw all to him as Jesus said in John 12:32 which says, "And I, if I be lifted up from the earth, will draw all men unto me." And the reward of yielding to this draw is shown in John 6:44 which says, "No man can come to me, except the

Father which hath sent me draw him: and I will raise him up at the last day." I truly believe that God has been drawing Tim, and now that he has made the trip to the altar I feel like he has reached the point where he will humble himself, and then he too will reap the reward of being raised up when Jesus comes back to take his bride home.

The singing continued for a few minutes until he raised his head, wiping the tears from his eyes. The four of us stood up as the choir started to wind down, and we all embraced – three of us awaiting Tim to say something. James handed Tim a tissue, and asked if everything was ok.

"I don't think I've ever been this ok." He said smiling.

"Did you get things worked out with the Lord?" James asked.

"Let me just put it this way. Do you think you could fit one more baptism into your schedule today?"

Carmen and I both burst out in tears of Joy, and amen was being shouted from all over the church.

James turned around to the congregation – smiling – holding his hand up in praise and asked, "Well, church….Can we fit one more baptism in today?"

Everyone continued shouting 'Amen', and 'Praise the Lord'. I don't think there was a dry eye in the building as people started coming down to the altar giving out hugs, and congratulating Tim. I couldn't help but give them a few hugs myself. I was so proud of how far these two had come in our short time together, but as I said before….the Lord knows what he's doing.

The rest of the service – including the baptism – went wonderfully. One of the young men in the church even loaned Tim a spare jogging suit to wear, since he hadn't planned on getting wet today, and everyone left the church rejoicing the fact that Jesus had brought one of his lost sheep into the fold.

Tim, Carmen, and I decided to go out for a late lunch, or early dinner – however you want to look at it – so that we could cherish a few more minutes together before I had to make my ascent back to higher altitudes. We had a very pleasant fellowship, and Tim reiterated many times how good he felt, and how thankful he was that we had crossed paths. Carmen was her usual cheerful self, and I could see the gleam in her eyes, as she was obviously thrilled that they could now start a new Christian life together.

As things came to a close it brought back memories of our first goodbyes, and this one was not going to be any easier, however, this time we promised to call more often, and I told them if they ever chose to head my way for vacation, they had to stay at my place at least one night.

We have kept in touch since then, in fact I think we talk at least once every couple of weeks, and they come up for revival at my church as I go to Mableton for theirs. Witnessing to them was not only helpful to them, but it was a growing experience for me as well, since Shirley was always the outspoken one in the family. It's a shame that many witnessing experiences are missed, because of so many different reasons, but it shouldn't be that way. A Christian should love God, and to love God means to love others, so we should have a desire in our hearts to share what we have with others so they can have that promise of eternal life as we do.

As I said before, witnessing is not always easy, and it doesn't always turn out the way we think it should; some are going to accept it as a gesture of love and kindness, and others are going to reject us along with God as they always have, but that shouldn't stop us from at least trying to plant that seed. If we are shunned by those who reject us, or lose people who pretend to be our friends then so be it. The apostles would rejoice to be counted worthy of persecution for the sake of Jesus Christ, and so should we.

I'm going to leave you with one final verse, and thought. John 3:16 says, "For God so loved the world, that he gave his only begotten Son, that whosoever believeth in him should not perish, but have everlasting life." I want you to think about what this is saying. It takes a tremendous amount of love to even consider giving your life for someone else, especially if the one you give it for has no respect or appreciation for you. This is exactly what Jesus has done for us. He not only gave his life for those who are kind, and live good honest lives, but he also died for all those who slap him in the face every chance they get by living the immoral self centered lives they've chosen. Forgiveness and salvation are there for everyone if they only choose to believe, and repent. Let's not waste our time that he's given us on this earth by standing by unconcerned of the people who need to know and understand what he's done for them. Study God's word – pray without ceasing –go out there and spread the gospel of Jesus Christ.

The End

Acknowledgments

First of all I want to give thanks to my Lord and Savior Jesus Christ who gave everything so that a wretch like me could be saved from the punishment I deserve. I thank him for putting the desire in my heart to learn more about him, and develop the relationship with him that has given me more fulfillment in my life than I could have ever imagined. If it wasn't for his desire to reconcile ungrateful and unworthy sinful people, then there would be no hope whatsoever for the human race. There's just no way for me to ever thank him enough for what he's done for me.

I would like to thank my parents for raising me in a Christian home, and doing their best to lead by example. I know there had to be many instances where they questioned whether or not anything was sinking in, but they never gave up and always kept their faith. The Bible says that parents should raise their kids in the way they should go and when they're old they won't depart from it, which testifies that the reward can be later down the road in their children's lives. Even though I may not have acted like it at times, their values did sink in and made an extreme difference in my life.

There's no way I could go without thanking my beautiful wife Stacy for backing me up in all of this. There were many times where I was studying and writing instead of spending time with her but she understood. Not only was she understanding, but she was wholly supportive of this venture. Enough can't be said about having a spouse that wants to follow Jesus and is willing to do whatever it takes to do his will. When she says to me "You need to do what you need to do." I know she understands that I'm trying to follow the Lord and she doesn't want to obstruct that in any way, so thank you baby.

My friend John has to be mentioned as well because, whether he knew it or not, he was a major contributor to my desire to learn. During many of our late night discussions, the questions he brought to my attention made me realize just how little I really knew about the faith I claimed to have, and it engendered a desire to always be ready to give an answer about my faith.

Last but certainly not least, I would like to thank the Answers in Genesis organization whos website, books, and media materials were instrumental in helping me discover the truth about science, and how real science doesn't contradict Biblical teachings, but confirms its teachings. These men and women have dedicated themselves to equipping Christians all over the world, with the tools needed to defend our faith and counteract the fallacies which permeate our culture. I appreciate everything these men and women do and stand for, and wish them the best in all things. I encourage anyone who is willing to test their belief or unbelief, to go to their website at – answersingenesis.org – and see what information is available to those willing to see.

Made in the USA
Columbia, SC
05 February 2018